WRECKING
BALL
RELATIONSHIPS

WRECKING BALL RELATIONSHIPS

How to Identify, Live With or Leave the Narcissist in Your Life

LYNN CATALANO, ESQ.

Published by Lynn Catalano Speaks
WWW.LYNNCATALANO.COM

Printed in the United States of America

Library of Congress Control Number: 2022900106
Library of Congress Cataloging-in-Publication data
Catalano, Lynn W.
Wrecking Ball Relationships: how to identify, live with or leave the narcissist in your life / Lynn W. Catalano p. cm.
ISBN: 979-8-9855540-0-7 pbk
ISBN: 979-8-9855540-1-4 ebk

1. Psychology. 2. Narcissism. 3. Interpersonal relationships.
First Edition

10 9 8 7 6 5 4 3 2 1

*This book is dedicated to Joseph, Madeline,
and Allison for believing in me.
I carry your heart in my heart.*

*To my mother, my first supporter,
always in my heart.*

TABLE OF CONTENTS

CHAPTER 1   *Am I Being Punk'd?*   1

CHAPTER 2   *How to Identify a Narcissist*   15

CHAPTER 3   *Are Narcissists Born or Bred?*   31

CHAPTER 4   *The Wrecking Ball Demolition Plan*   45

CHAPTER 5   *The Ruin of Rage Storms*   57

CHAPTER 6   *Toxic Bosses Cause Chaos*   71

CHAPTER 7   *Covert Narcissists Wreak Quiet Havoc*   89

CHAPTER 8   *Unstable Destruction: When Your Sibling is a Narcissist*   105

CHAPTER 9   *Gaslighting: More like Pouring Gas on the Fire*   119

CHAPTER 10   *Romantic Heart-Wrenching Relationships that Ravage*   135

CHAPTER 11   *Emotional Grenades*   151

CHAPTER 12   *The Silent Treatment Damages & Desolates*   165

CHAPTER 13   *Shock & Awe*   183

CHAPTER 14   *Moving On: Avoid the Demolition Plan*   199

ACKNOWLEDGMENTS   217

GLOSSARY   219

RESOURCE GUIDE   235

HOW TO CONNECT   249

WRECKING
BALL
RELATIONSHIPS

1

AM I BEING PUNK'D?

" ... you can't spit in our faces and then tell us it's raining."

The Evening Post (NY)

My mother was just buried a few days ago. I'm in the car with my father as he drives, still trying to process her sudden death and the ramifications. Everything is different. It just can't be real. I felt like I was living in an alternate universe somehow. It's a beautiful, sunny, August day. I can't remember where we were going. My mother's funeral was packed with people, it was standing room only. It was held at our longtime synagogue. At least 300 people came to pay their respects to her and all of us.

My father cocks his head and abruptly says, *"I just don't know where you'll hold my funeral. If that many people showed up for mom, I can't imagine how big a place you'll need for me."*

What? Was I being punk'd? Was this grief talking? Where did this come from?

Recently, someone pointed out I grew up with a life of emotional privilege. I'd never heard this term before. I always knew I was loved. My mother said so multiple times a day. As an only child, I felt like the center of her universe. In college, I realized how idyllic my childhood was compared to others.

"You own everything that happened to you. Tell your stories. If people wanted you to write warmly about them, they should have behaved better."

Anne Lamott

I never doubted my "inner resources." Mom defined this as the certain knowledge that you're loved, valued, and important. Every day I left home ready to tackle new challenges, feeling confident.

But now I found myself questioning everything. My journey learning about narcissism began because what I thought were feelings of loss and grief from my father slowly turned into confusion. I was doing the best I could to deal with my mother's death, raise two young daughters, be a wife, and work full-time.

As time progressed, I didn't understand what was happening with my father.

Was I going crazy? Nothing felt normal or at least nothing felt as it had my whole life until then. It felt like up was down and black was white. This couldn't be right, could it? My father was a person I depended on, showed respect, and who held me to the highest standard. He wasn't like this before, or was he? I was completely thrown off balance. I spent a lot of time asking myself questions that didn't have any answers.

DO YOU FEEL YOU'RE GOING CRAZY BECAUSE OF A NARCISSIST? DO YOU FEEL:

- *Belittled?*
- *Lied to and when you question it, they get upset?*
- *A sense of self-doubt, in fact doubts about everything.*
- *Stressed and anxious being around them?*
- *They've been wearing a mask and then suddenly taken it off?*

I felt these things too. I sought information and researched the behaviors. Googling his behaviors to figure out what was happening brought up huge red flags that something was seriously wrong. I kept thinking of something to compare his actions.

Wrecking balls serve as the quintessential icon of demolition. A wrecking ball is a massive ball of steel weighing up to 12,000 pounds. It's suspended from a crane and swung into a building, with its sheer weight, inertia, and gravity doing the work to demolish the building. I felt like a wrecking ball was demolishing my emotions, my stability, and my relationship.

This is what it feels like to have a relationship with a narcissist. It's a wrecking ball relationship.

I hope after reading this book, it will help bring you clarity. While discovering more about his perplexing, upsetting behaviors, I realized this was narcissism. I'd never even thought about it before. I read and listened to every resource available on narcissism. Then I went to therapy to learn coping skills to co-exist with him. The hits kept coming from him and I continued feeling like a contestant on the MTV reality show "Punk'd." I was only half-joking when I started looking for hidden cameras.

The trail of breadcrumbs was there, if only I could see them. We kept chalking up his odd behavior to grief. Long before hearing the term narcissism, I was familiar with family who behaved differently, I noticed as a young teen and pointed it out to mother. This part of our family can be described with the iconic greeting from Bette Midler's characterization of CC Bloom in the movie Beaches: *"But enough about me, let's talk about you ... what do you think of me?"*

THIS BOOK IS IDEAL FOR YOU IF YOUR NARCISSIST:

- *Lies to you and then gets upset when you question them*
- *Uses tactics like the Silent Treatment to torment you*
- *Turns the tables and makes themselves the victim*

AS YOU READ, YOU'LL MEET:

- *Jessica, who became like a private investigator to discover nothing about her life with her narcissist was real.*

- *Kim, whose narcissist tried to triangulate family members for their own benefit.*

- *Jake, whose narcissist is constantly competing, no matter who realizes it.*

- *Patricia, who grew up walking on eggshells because her narcissist might explode.*

- *Beth, who eventually loathed her narcissist so much, she hated his breathing.*

- *Dominique, who thought her narcissist's womanizing ways were behind him.*

My mother created a loving home atmosphere, during the first thirty-nine years of my life. I never realized the connection between my father, and I *was* my mother. She was the hub, the facilitator, the translator, the moderator. With her there, we didn't need to communicate directly. I never noticed this until she was gone.

Problems between me and him began shortly after she died. Suddenly it occurred to me, I didn't know how to communicate with him. I expected him to behave with the same kindness, love and caring my mother expressed. He expected praise, reassurance, and an enabler of his narcissistic ways. Without constantly building up his ego, as she did during the 40-plus years they were married, he wasn't the person I thought he was.

Funny, my husband and I have raised our daughters in a family filled with an abundance of emotional privilege. We lavish love and acceptance on each other. We don't leave the house or end a phone call without saying I love you. I think this would make my mother proud.

So now in the era of Trump, narcissism has become a word on everyone's lips. Does it seem like everyone's a narcissist these days? Do people almost use the term "narcissist" generically?

According to a New York Times article, "It has become the go-to diagnosis by columnists, bloggers, and television psychologists. A term that has deep roots in psychoanalytic literature appears to have become a popular descriptor so bloated as to have been rendered meaningless." This was written years before Donald Trump ever came down the golden escalator and set foot on the political stage.

Returning to the 1980s, terms like "narcissistic," "insane," "psychotic," "hysterical" and other psychological terminology began seeping into our popular vernacular.

A Washington Post article surmised how Trump would fare on the Narcissistic Personality Quiz. Psychologists use this 40-question assessment to measure the personality disorder. The article started by listing the first statement on the quiz "I have a natural talent for influencing people." People taking the quiz are asked whether they agree or disagree with this statement: "If I ruled the world, it would be a far better place." Typical narcissists genuinely believe these statements. The article inferred if Trump took the test, he'd boast about his high score.

People today throw around the term narcissist for anyone who exhibits self-centered behavior. Since our last president left the Oval Office, anyone who attracts attention is branded a narcissist.

Here's a fun example: As I was learning about narcissism, I invited my father over for dinner. I recently hung new family photographs, enlarged, and framed on a wall. There were five photographs in total: he was in two of them. He came to dinner, and I asked if he liked the photos.

He replied, "*I like that one and that one,*" pointing only to the photos he was in.

You just can't make this stuff up. Punk'd again.

At our youngest daughter's bat mitzvah, things weren't good between us, but I invited him anyway. Not wanting him to miss this important occasion, I thought it might be an opportunity for reconciliation. Maybe extending an olive branch of peace would bring him around. Maybe he'd want to start a conversation or even apologize. He didn't see it that way. At the party, he called over the professional photographer and asked her to take special photos. You're thinking he wanted photos with his granddaughters or other family members– nope. He asked the photographer to take candid photos of him, walking, laughing, all him. Only him. Yes, where are the hidden cameras?

I felt discouraged upon learning this disorder is unlike any other. There's no magic pill or therapy. Most people who suffer from it never seek help. So, it's extremely difficult to be in a relationship with a narcissist. You've noticed that too, right?

According to the same New York Times article exploring narcissism, "today, therapists say, patients who receive a diagnosis of the disorder remain among the most challenging to help because they often believe their problem is that others never sufficiently recognize how special they are. In childhood they had been deprived of essential emotional sustenance; as adults, their arrogance, sense of entitlement and exhibitionistic tendencies spring from the deepest humiliation."

YOU MAY ALREADY BE AWARE OF HOW NARCISSISTS CONDUCT THEMSELVES.

- *They have a demeanor of superiority.*
- *Their speech is demanding, argumentative, competitive.*
- *Everything is a competition.*
- *They talk over people, frequently interrupting.*
- *They usually withhold vital information.*

It's all about control. They won't answer direct questions. Instead, they'll deflect and turn the tables and suddenly become the victim. They bully and interrogate to get the information they want. My father would go into something I came to know as his "narcissistic spin" or "narc spin." This happened every time he perceived something as offensive or didn't get what he wanted. He would become very quiet if around others and then stop talking to me immediately after for an undetermined period of time. This almost feels like an extended temper tantrum and acts a predecessor to a narcissistic rage storm. You'll read more on these rage storms in Chapter 5. Often their verbal attack is so swift, victims don't have time to properly respond. How do you deal with this?

Trauma early in their life caused them to develop a way of living in a false reality with no healthy boundaries.

WHAT ARE TYPICAL THINGS NARCISSISTS SAY?

- *"Oh, you're misinterpreting. It was just a joke. I was being funny. Can't you take a joke?"*

- *"Are you calling me a liar? Are you saying that didn't happen?"*

- *"That's not how it happened. This is how it happened. You're remembering wrong."*

- *"People recognize me all the time and I don't remember anybody's name."*

- *"I get invited to so many things."*

- *"It's been extremely hard for me. You never think about how hard it's been on me and how things are for me."*

- ⊚ *"Communication goes two ways."*
- ⊚ *"You always overreact!"*
- ⊚ *"You've always had a vivid imagination!"*
- ⊚ *"I love you, but ... "*
- ⊚ *"This back and forth is making me sick. I'm not going to make myself sick over this debate with you."*
- ⊚ *"Stop twisting everything. Stop reading into things."*

WHO GETS TO DECIDE IF YOU'VE SUFFERED EMOTIONAL ABUSE?

We're living in a time of destigmatizing mental illness and being radically aware of our emotional pain. So, it's important to note people who deal with narcissists on a regular basis struggle with constant emotional pain. You may not understand what's happening or you're made to feel you're overly sensitive, inflexible, and unaccepting.

On these pages you'll find detailed information about how narcissists act, things they say and their typical behaviors. But what about you? What about the victims of their abuse? How does their behavior make you feel? If you're reading this book, you've felt the effects of the wrecking ball.

RELATIONSHIPS WITH NARCISSISTS MAKE PEOPLE FEEL LIKE THEY'RE:

- *Going crazy*
- *Lost and unsure of things you counted on*
- *Out of control*
- *Confused and helpless*
- *Disrespected and disregarded*
- *Overwhelmed*
- *Filled with shame*
- *Experiencing a devastation they didn't know was possible*

Who's the narcissist in your life? How have they impacted you? By sharing the stories of people who've experienced similar situations, I hope to bring you a sense of ease. You're not alone and you're not going crazy. I hope this book helps clarify the issues you've experienced around narcissism and make clear who this person is and the damage they're capable of creating.

You'll notice humor throughout the book, or rather dark humor. It's a coping mechanism instead of crying constantly or plunging into deep depression. My heart is broken. I always believed I could depend on him as dad. The experience was so hurtful, humor helped make coping easier.

WHO WILL BE THERE FOR YOU? WHAT WILL HELP YOU SURVIVE YOUR TOXIC RELATIONSHIP?

A lighthouse is a metaphor that represents a beacon of hope as it guides the way for vessels at sea. As you read, you'll find your own lighthouses. These amazing non-judgmental people will listen and express empathy for what you're enduring.

My husband Joseph was not just a lighthouse, he was a lifeline. Three other close friends were amazingly supportive. It doesn't take a big circle of people, just a few can make an enormous difference.

This book isn't a tell-all, I'm not airing dirty laundry. I went through a tough time trying to determine what was happening. After learning about narcissism, my childhood finally made sense. There were many "a-ha moments."

The aim of this book is to share my story and help you find answers. There is comfort in other people's stories with their narcissistic experiences. Learning from others made me feel I wasn't alone. Many people kindly volunteered to share their stories. You'll find answers and coping strategies to deal with the narcissist in your life.

Typical narcissists exhibit certain behaviors on repeat – deny, deflect, lie – all to the tune of "Razzle Dazzle" from the musical *Chicago*. Whether the narcissist is a parent, a boyfriend, a spouse, a sibling, or a boss; They love-bomb you and praise you to get you to do something. If you go off the narcissist's script, they jump onstage to perform their dance.

"How can they hear the truth above the roar?" Ironically, I've long referred to this as the "Narcissist's Theme Song" and a recent journalist referred to it as the "Theme Song for the Trump Reality Show." This feels like their narc spin at work.

WHAT WILL YOU LEARN?

Narcissists say things to provoke, confuse, manipulate, and hurt. Narcissists want you to do certain things and then get mad when you do them. It's like you make a time to meet, the narcissist is early and then gets mad when you're on time. They blame you for your reaction to their disrespect. It's a constant manipulation. Unfortunately, there's some truth in their jokes.

Since growing up with a narcissistic parent, empathy became my superpower. Empaths tend to feel guilt for not going along with the narcissist's directions. It's not selfish to set boundaries or make yourself more difficult to manipulate. I was confused and lost because things weren't as they seemed. Once I learned what was wrong it wasn't difficult to learn how to adapt.

This book isn't about someone in your life making a mistake that hurt you. This is about a pattern of behavior that's disrespectful, demeaning, and detrimental to you over time. It feels like alternating water torture, drip, drip, drip, and head-on cruel and unusual punishment. Here comes the wrecking ball again ...

I've implemented changes to better deal with the toxicity. It's been like earning a graduate degree after the experience. Part of it was learning I wasn't going crazy. Something indeed was wrong. Upon learning what was happening, I hope the journey helps you.

You aren't alone or being too sensitive. This book will help you identify the toxic people in your life and navigate them. Some readers can leave and eliminate the toxicity from their life. Other readers, like me, can't leave. A parent is still a parent, no matter what. Don't pretend these people can change, they won't. You'll need to change, adapt, and grow to protect yourself. I hope this book sets you on the right path to a healthy mental and emotional place and better relationships.

2

HOW TO IDENTIFY A NARCISSIST

"Half the harm that is done in this world is due to people who want to feel important ... They justify it because they are absorbed in the endless struggle to think well of themselves."

T.S. Eliot

WHAT IS A NARCISSIST? WHAT DOES IT MEAN?

It may surprise you to know the clinical diagnosis of narcissism has only existed for about 50 years, but the behavioral patterns reach back much farther. Significant analysis of narcissism with descriptions of the characteristics and tendencies is revealing. In this chapter, you'll discover the answers to the questions above.

Emotional Intelligence, while a relatively new concept, provides a provocative contrast to narcissism. When illustrated in conversation the difference is compelling. One analysis I'll discuss breaks down a diagnosis of narcissism into easy-to-understand terms. I've also included an exploration of the most celebrated narcissist in recent years.

HISTORY

The story of Narcissus originated from Greek mythology. The son of the river g-d Cephissus and the nymph Liriope, Narcissus was a handsome, egotistical young man. He looked like the modern-day Fabio, famous for his provocative images on the cover of many romance novels. Imagine Narcissus, strolling around with an expansive, hairless chest exposed to show off his six-pack abs, with flowing, blonde hair lifting in the breeze and eyes as blue as the ocean. He seemed to walk in slow motion casually flipping his long locks out of his face, as all the women who witnessed him swooned. It's difficult to see how the lovely nymph, Echo, could resist his charms.

In contrast to his stunning beauty, his story is quite depressing. After rejecting Echo, his punishment was a sentence to love only himself. He fell in love with his image upon seeing his visage in a pool of water. He was completely mesmerized. Nothing could tear him away from his reflection. So smitten was he with himself, he found it impossible to leave the water's edge and stop gazing at himself until he eventually wasted away.

Throughout history philosophers have explored the concept of excessive vanity and unusually self-absorbed people. The term "hubris" originates from the Greek "hybris" and means pride or arrogance, and, in Greek tragedy, it refers to an excess of ambition and pride, finally causing the transgressor's ruin.

It wasn't until the early 1900s when the topic of narcissism attracted significance in the study of psychoanalysis. In 1911, Otto Rank, an Austrian psychoanalyst, published one of the earliest known descriptions of narcissism. Rank connected it to self-admiration and vanity. In 1914, Sigmund Freud, the father of psychoanalysis, published a paper titled, "On Narcissism: An Introduction." He found narcissism a normal part of the human psyche and necessary for proper human development. However, most humans outgrow this primary narcissistic age, unless they don't, and they engage in a lifetime of self-absorption and vanity. They lose all sense of self. Freud famously said, "Whoever loves becomes humble. Those who love have, so to speak, pawned a part of their narcissism."

In the 1960s Austrian psychoanalysts Otto Kernberg and Heinz Kohut, helped draw more attention to and interest in narcissism through their publications on the topic. They believed adult narcissism begins in early childhood. They focused on the concept of early disturbances in parental relationships as the origin of adult narcissism. They went beyond Freud's theories coining the term "pathological narcissism." In 1967, Kernberg introduced the term "narcissistic personality structure." Then in 1968, Kohut coined the term "narcissistic personality disorder." Each had different theories about narcissism. Yet they both portrayed narcissists as people with unsatisfactory childhood relationships who have unhealthy views of self, resulting in grandiose ideals and arrogance as adults.

Finally, in 1980 the American Psychiatric Association officially recognized narcissistic personality disorder.

HOW TO IDENTIFY A NARCISSIST

Is it shocking to learn at least six percent of Americans suffer from Narcissistic Personality Disorder? Would it be even more shocking to learn almost 80 percent of them are men? Let that sink in – one out of sixteen people is a narcissist. That means we all run into them at some point in our lives. Some do severe damage in our relationships. Learning to identify this type of person will save you pain, agony and time.

The Diagnostic & Statistical Manual of Mental Disorders is the standard handbook used by healthcare professionals in the Americas and much of the world. It's recognized as the authoritative guide to the diagnosis of mental disorders. It states Narcissistic Personality Disorder (NPD) is a pattern of self-centered, egotistical behavior destructive to others. Narcissists put their needs before others. They tend to step on people who get in their way and even go out of their way to hurt them. The most important characteristics of NPD are grandiosity, seeking excessive admiration and a lack of empathy. There is no cure for NPD and most people affected by it are blissfully unaware they suffer from it. So, they don't seek help. The American Psychiatric Association defines narcissistic personality disorder as persistent grandiosity, a continuous desire for admiration, and a lack of empathy.

IT BEGINS IN EARLY ADULTHOOD AND IS SEEN IN PEOPLE WITH AT LEAST FIVE OF THE FOLLOWING CHARACTERISTICS:

- *An exaggerated sense of self-importance. They expect to be recognized as superior without matching achievements.*

- *A preoccupation with fantasies of unlimited success, power, brilliance, beauty, or ideal love.*

- *Believes he/she is "special" and should only associate with other special high-status people or institutions.*

- *Requires excessive admiration*

- *Has a strong sense of entitlement*

- *Selfishly takes advantage of others to achieve his own ends*

- *Lacks empathy or genuine concern for others*

- *Is often envious or believes others are envious of him*

- *Shows arrogant, haughty, patronizing, or contemptuous behavior*

In 2013, The American Psychiatric Association set out a model characterizing narcissistic personality disorder as an impairment in personality functioning, seen as troubles in at least two of the following areas:

- *Individuality – or identity; There are significant ups and downs between extremes of inflated or deflated self-appraisal and fluctuations regulating emotions.*

- *Self-direction – Goals are set to gain approval or compete with others; standards are unreasonably high when one sees oneself as exceptional. There is no real "self" in self-direction as it is based on others.*

- *Empathy – The ability to recognize or identify with the feelings and needs of others is severely impaired.*

- *Closeness – or intimacy; They don't have many friends as their relationships are largely superficial. Relationships are primarily used for personal gain.*

The Mayo Clinic explains some typical behaviors common in NPD.

THEY:

- *Monopolize conversations and belittle or look down on people they consider inferior, and they consider almost everyone inferior.*

- *Have trouble handling anything they view as criticism. They often:*

- *Become impatient or angry when they don't receive special treatment*
- *Have significant interpersonal problems and easily feel slighted*
- *React with rage or contempt, belittling others to appear superior*
- *Have difficulty regulating emotions and behavior*
- *Experience major problems dealing with stress and adapting to change*
- *Feel depressed and moody if they fall short of perfection*
- *Harbor feelings of insecurity, shame, vulnerability, and humiliation*

The Mayo Clinic also recognizes possible causes for NPD acknowledging what causes narcissistic personality disorder is unknown. You'll read more about causes of narcissism in Chapter 3.

IT MAY BE LINKED TO:

- *Environment – a mismatch in parent-child relationships with excessive adoration or criticism, poorly attuned to the child's experience.*
- *Genetics – inherited characteristics*
- *Neurobiology – refers to the connection between the brain and behavior and thinking.*

They continue to recognize possible complications of NPD.

THESE CONDITIONS INCLUDE:

- *Relationship difficulties*
- *Problems at work or school*
- *Depression and anxiety*
- *Physical health problems*
- *Drug or alcohol misuse*
- *Suicidal thoughts or behavior*

HOW IS EMOTIONAL INTELLIGENCE THE OPPOSITE OF NARCISSISTIC PERSONALITY DISORDER?

The term Emotional Intelligence (EI) was first published in 1990 by researchers but became almost a household phrase after Dan Goleman's 1996 book *Emotional Intelligence*.

Emotional Intelligence is defined as "the ability to recognize, understand and manage our own emotions and recognize, understand and influence the emotions of others."

Leadership experts have long focused on the importance of emotional intelligence and what it brings to organizations. If you look at the two concepts, emotional intelligence versus narcissistic personality disorder, the differences are startling, and appear as opposites.

Can both exist in one person simultaneously? Some people feel it's possible. Emotionally intelligent people engage in healthy behavior including mindfulness, empathy, self-control, confidence, self-respect, and a minimum of arrogance. Narcissists employ only confidence, self-respect, and arrogance with little or no regard, tolerance, or patience for others. A balance exists within emotionally intelligent people not present in narcissists.

Narcissistic Personality Disorder	Emotional Intelligence
Does not care about anyone else's emotions	Recognize & understand our emotions and the emotions of others
Cannot demonstrate or feel empathy	Exhibits empathy
Tantrums, blame storms and rage outbursts	Regulation of one's own emotions
Overconfident of one's abilities	Practical in self-assessment of skills

Imagine a party where you encounter a person who's a known narcissist, and another person known for a high level of emotional intelligence. Perhaps it's a conversation between former President Trump and Oprah Winfrey. Media and psychologists around the world have nonprofessionally/non-clinically diagnosed the former President from before he was elected until he left the Oval Office as a narcissist. However, it's unknown if he's ever been clinically diagnosed. Oprah Winfrey is well known for her empathy and ability to understand people. She's used her platform for good for years. How would the conversation go?

DT: "I hate this place. They always screw up my order. They hire the worst servers too."

OW: "I've been trying to meet with you. I'm fascinated in your opinion about our crisis of confidence in the U.S. today. How does it make you feel?"

DT: "I feel parched. I need a drink, and no one's asked me what I want!"

OW: "I was referring to the current tension between races and classes today in our country."

DT: "Have you been to my new exclusive private club in Chicago? It's right around the corner from my hotel. They only invite the biggest names to join."

OW: "I don't think I'm familiar with that club. I'm not really into exclusive. I enjoy more inclusive places these days."

DT: "I see so-and-so over there. He just sold a huge portion of his business. He really should come over and talk to me."

OW: "I don't know who he is."

DT: "I'm ticked off about being shut out of that special VIP award. Everything's so political. Just watch, I'll be back. I promise you that."

OW: "I didn't ask you about politics or your future. I just wanted your opinion about society since you left office."

This is a peek into a typical exchange with a narcissist. They aren't interested in you or anyone else unless it advances their cause. They have a desire to be desired. They want people to come see them. They also feel the service, taste, appearance, or sound of something is never up to their standards. If they feel an ounce of disappointment about any one of those things, the narcissist prepares themselves to dislike that restaurant, food, drink, or server next time. They openly share their dislike or disappointment. The narcissist rarely asks open-ended questions. They mostly engage in conversation about what they've done because they're special, important people.

The empath or high emotionally intelligent person is just seeking to have a conversation. They don't care about all these distractions and noise. They ask deep, thoughtful questions and don't receive answers from the narcissist.

I share this imaginary party scene to demonstrate what might occur between two people who are opposites on the scale between people with NPD and high EI. After former President Trump gives a speech, his wife, Melania, calls to praise him. Former adviser to the First Lady, Stephanie Winston Wolkoff claims *she was always his first phone call.* He requires constant praise, recognition, reassurance, and reward.

What would it look like if Oprah Winfrey had a similar conversation at a party with a well-known person who has high emotional intelligence like billionaire Richard Branson?

OW: "Well hello Sir Richard Branson. How are you this evening?"

RB: "Please don't use the 'Sir' title. I don't need it. I'm excellent tonight. How are you, Oprah?"

OW: "Thanks for asking. I'm doing very well tonight. What would you say is the secret to your success?"

RB: "I believe the people who've helped my ideas take shape are the lynchpin to my success. The best designed business plan will come to nothing if it isn't carried out by enthusiastic, passionate staff."

OW: "Fascinating. This global pandemic is awful. You lost your mother to Covid-19. Was she proud of you?"

RB: "My mum was a force of nature. She was healthy and happy before this wretched virus. She taught me not to take myself so seriously."

OW: "What activities are most important to you these days?"

RB: "Journaling. I've found it is a great way to reflect and I've learned I love writing."

OW: "It was a pleasure speaking with you tonight."

RB: "The pleasure was all mine."

Anyone eavesdropping on this conversation would take away the genuineness and connection between the two. Richard Branson immediately plays down his title. He answers Oprah's questions frankly and credits others with his success. He speaks about his mother as keeping him grounded and is developing a hobby which helps him reflect. These are all habits of a highly emotional, intelligent person. Quite the contrary from the previous conversation.

There's a deep-seated insecurity in narcissists that must be constantly fed and bolstered. While they appear to possess high self-confidence, it's all a show of smoke and mirrors. They depend on people to pump them up, so they feel reassured. As shown in the second conversation, there is no need for this pretense among people who are both emotionally intelligent. There is an easy patter of conversation with mutual respect between Oprah and Richard that didn't exist between Oprah and Donald.

WHAT HAVE YOU LEARNED?

While Greek mythology tells the story of Narcissus thousands of years ago, narcissistic personality disorder was only recognized 60 years ago and diagnosed in the last 40 years. As a nation, Americans were a captive audience to the former President's actions, words, and tendencies. It was difficult to ignore the narcissistic characteristics identified by experts in our former President.

Psychologists agree President Trump fits the psychological profile of a narcissist just as we might describe a public figure or celebrity who spends their days drinking alcohol as having an alcohol problem. George Simon, a clinical psychologist who conducts academic seminars on manipulative behavior says, "Trump is so classic that I'm archiving video clips of him to use in workshops because there's no better example of narcissism. Otherwise, I'd have to hire actors and write vignettes. He's like a dream come true."

Narcissists all share some basic characteristics. They must always be the most important person in the room and their needs must come first. They rarely ask open-ended questions as they don't care about the answer. They love when you ask questions about themselves. "What was it like when you achieved your goal, walked on the moon, solved world peace?"

The sooner a problem is identified, the sooner a course can be charted designing a solution or remedy for yourself; whether you decide to learn coping mechanisms and stay or, cut and run. The better educated you are about the problem, the easier it will be to figure out what to do. Unfortunately, with narcissists, you must always keep your guard up, be on defense, hyper-aware of every word exchanged. This often makes the relationship feel like a chess game.

As I looked for answers, trying to figure out what was happening in my life, I looked up many personality disorders in the DSM-V. It wasn't until I read the symptoms and characteristics of narcissistic personality disorder, did I realize my father had a serious problem. Consequently, I realized I had a serious problem.

It's essential to remember although these people have big personalities, demand attention and entitlement in arrogant ways, they're deeply flawed, shameful people with poor self-esteem. Their thin veneer of confidence is an elaborate ruse to convince the world they're the smartest and the best.

After years of emotional abuse, it's difficult for me to have much sympathy for my father. However, I see the cracks in the foundation of his personality. I also see the roots of his low self-esteem. This helped me devise coping skills so I could not only survive our relationship but also live a happy, functional, and fulfilling life.

Walking on eggshells with narcissists is no longer how I choose to live. In fact, now I spend as little time as possible with the narcissist in my life after years of emotional abuse.

3

ARE NARCISSISTS BORN OR BRED?

"It is not attention that the child is seeking, but love."

~ Sigmund Freud

A recent Business Insider article listed 24 behavioral traits successful kids have in common. Ironically, 15 of these behaviors are about a child's emotional well-being, building strong inner resources, and high emotional intelligence. This list shouldn't be surprising today. Most of us are familiar with the general behaviors which contribute to strong emotional child development and a well-adjusted adult and which behaviors fall short of that goal.

Nature and nurture work together synergistically as equally important teammates in childhood and brain development. The age-old debate as to what is nature vs. nurture in child development continues to this day. Traits that develop from nature include the genetic predisposition or biological makeup of a person like an eye, hair, and skin color. Nurture is represented by the physical world which influences the nature of a person.

For many years, scientists have researched how a child's environment affects their development into becoming an emotionally stable, kind, well-balanced person or if that child grows into someone less stable, kind, or well-balanced. After researching narcissism, interviewing many survivors of narcissistic abuse, and putting together the pieces of their stories, I came up with what makes a narcissist. If there was a mathematical equation showing how a narcissist is created, I think it would look a lot like the formula below:

Emotionally unavailable parent(s) + emotional neglect of child + overindulgence = narcissistic person

The parent doesn't have to be a narcissist themselves to raise one. They just need to be emotionally unavailable. What does it mean to be emotionally available? Sharing yourself with another person and developing an authentic connection, an attunement to their needs characterizes emotional availability. According to an article from moms.com, "when it comes to emotionally available mothers, this means that you actively do things to bond with your child and make them an important part of your life." Over the years, research has supported the necessity that all children need emotionally available parents to survive. We know children can survive without emotionally available parents, however as a result they must adapt, and it affects them in different ways. When a child lacks this emotional availability, they're more likely to develop their maladaptive coping skills of insecurity, fear, no true sense of self, and possible mental illnesses including narcissism. PsychCentral.com identified certain behaviors often demonstrated by emotionally unavailable parents.

SIGNS OF HAVING AN EMOTIONALLY UNAVAILABLE PARENT:

- *Rigidity (unwillingness to be flexible when needed),*

- *Low-stress tolerance (inability to tolerate stress maturely),*

- *Emotional instability with aggression (anger outbursts characterized by threats of physical aggression, suicidal gesture, cutting behaviors, or other acts of self-harm),*

- *Poor boundaries (desiring to be their child's friend instead of a parent),*

- *Unstable relationships (multiple partners or friends who create more trouble than peace),*

- *Looking for accolades, recognition, or support at all costs) among many other characteristics.*

The list above is eerily similar to the characteristics listed back in Chapter 2 identifying narcissists. Narcissists possess all those characteristics and more because of their emotionally unavailable upbringing, lack of emotional development, and attachment. This conclusion isn't derived from scientific research. This is my subjective and yet highly logical conclusion. I hope some psychological research team of scientists tests my analysis to prove the theory. If a child grows up and develops into an adult with one or both emotionally unavailable parents, don't "see" the child, pay attention to him/her, support, or affirm or lovingly cherish him or her, then there's a good possibility the child will develop into a narcissist.

Narcissists never develop a secure sense of self. They may look overindulged in material things, but they're devoid of essential emotional attachment.

Interestingly, all narcissists are emotionally unavailable but not all emotionally unavailable people are narcissists.

HOW DOES NEGLECT AFFECT CHILD DEVELOPMENT?

I'm not referring to the type of neglect where a child doesn't receive the necessities of life: including food, water, shelter, and clothing. I'm referring to a much more passive type of neglect, emotional neglect. The child's basic survival needs are met, but the parent is emotionally unavailable to the child.

There is no physical affection, actually very little affection at all. This may be due to a parent with a fragile mental state, depression, or illness. Whatever the reason for the neglect, the parent does not or cannot provide a necessary foundation for the child to develop good emotional intelligence. The child grows up relatively ignored and left to his or her own devices.

Former U.S. President Donald Trump's mother was ill for most of his early formative years, in and out of the hospital. She wasn't present to provide that critical bonding, nurturing, loving environment so necessary for healthy emotional development.

In Mary Trump's book, *Too Much and Never Enough*, she explains, "if we're lucky, we have, as infants and toddlers, at least one emotionally available parent who consistently fulfills our needs and responds to our desires for attention." Modern child development teaches the critical importance of the child bonding with a primary caregiver in the early years. This bonding creates the fundamental foundation of emotional safety and healthy development for the child throughout their life. This leads to higher emotional intelligence for the child who grows into an emotionally intelligent adult. Donald Trump never received this foundation from either parent.

In an article on goalcast.com, the six things parents unwittingly do to encourage the development of narcissistic traits are listed and include:

1. They use shame-based parenting

This is a negative reinforcement style of parenting using shame to stop children's behavior causing negative thoughts and feelings about themselves.

2. They shower their child with adoration

Too much of anything isn't a good thing. The narcissist child is both emotionally neglected and showered with general non-specific praise.

3. They don't coach their child on empathy

Children need to develop empathy or understand they're part of a big world. It's so important to help your child learn about other people's feelings and differences and to understand and appreciate our diversity.

4. Their love is conditional

Children who learn their value comes from their achievements or how they look or perform in sports are more likely to become narcissists.

5. They are emotionally unavailable–and compensate with material things

These kids may have gadgets and wonderful experiences and privileges but are given no opportunity to grow an emotional vocabulary or emotional self-awareness. This is just overindulging the kids.

6. They are bad role models

Do as I say, not as I do.

As adults, narcissists' emotions are almost frozen to their childhood emotions. They have similar reactions to children, as adults going into tantrums, throwing emotional grenades, giving the silent treatment, and punishing their offenders. They still seek revenge on offenders or those they deem as disloyal.

How does a child develop emotional intelligence? How do parents balance the good with the bad? If you possess emotional intelligence, will you avoid becoming a narcissist? I believe the answer is yes. Having emotional intelligence means learning how to regulate your own emotions, learning empathy, and most importantly, learning to recognize and value the emotions of others.

If an emotional connection is the antidote to narcissism, how do you act like parents? What do you do differently? In an investigative article on parenting, the Washington Post examined seven positive things parents can do to raise emotionally intelligent children without narcissistic traits.

1. Love your kids, warts, and all. We must communicate to our children none of us are perfect. We need to show our children our love doesn't change when they try something and fail. We need to love our children for who they are right now. We love them no matter what, unconditionally.

2. Stick to the point with your praise. Be intentional and specific with your praise. Just telling them "Good job" isn't as meaningful as "you wrote an inciteful paper about the book." It's not about general adoration.

3. Praise the present. Don't make generalities in your praise as it makes the praise less important. Instead of saying "you always get good grades," say "you worked hard for your science grade." It's important to put the praise in the present. Children need to know their current achievement is being praised not their general accomplishments.

4. Be sparing, but not a miser, with your praise. Use praise appropriately and find a balance of when and how often. You don't want to raise a child who needs praise after every action.

5. Praise what is worthy of compliments. Too much praise devalues the praise and makes it less effective. The other extreme of giving too little praise affects the child's self-esteem. Praiseworthy actions and they'll be more powerful. This technique is important to show our children how their hard work pays off and they are not perfect.

6. Teach the Golden Rule. Teaching your children to treat others the way they'd like to be treated is the first step to learning empathy. Empathy is one of the key characteristics narcissists can't show. Teach your children they aren't the only ones on the planet and their actions have consequences on others.

7. Walk in their shoes. The more children are exposed to other ways of life, other colors, religions, and races, the more they understand and develop empathy. Use stories, movies,

and books to illustrate other perspectives and discuss these with your children. This knowledge helps children learn compassion and care about people other than just themselves.

Recognized as one of the most influential works of literature, the novel *Catcher in the Rye* was written by J.D. Salinger. The story focuses on Holden Caulfield, who suffers immense emotional trauma at the sudden loss of his brother. Holden doesn't have a support system as his parents are emotionally unavailable. He feels the adults in his life have failed him because he doesn't get the attention or comfort he needs from his parents. He tries to regulate his emotions after his brother's death but is unsuccessful. He experiences many failed connections with people and erratic thoughts. At its root, the story is a cautionary tale about what happens when mental illness and post-traumatic stress syndrome (PTSD) go untreated and the resulting misery. Holden's goal in life is to be a "catcher in the rye," a person who saves children from falling off a cliff. Critical reviews consider the book as a metaphor for leaving childhood and entering adulthood.

BREAKING THE CYCLE

Consequently, I realize now, one parent, my father, was emotionally unavailable throughout my childhood. However, my mother overcompensated for his inabilities with intense emotional privilege. I was unaware of it at the time. I only recently came across the term "emotional privilege." I now know he was not only emotionally unavailable but a narcissist as well. I've only briefly mentioned emotional privilege in earlier chapters as it influenced my expectations. I thought everyone received the level of parental attention, commitment, and devotion I received. Quick update, they did not. My mother created a loving, soft bubble filled with inner resources and self-confidence which gave me the courage and tenacity to try new things and conquer my goals.

How did she provide this foundation of emotional privilege? She methodically focused all her positive energy on her only child. Me. She didn't hover like today's helicopter mom. She didn't snoop, meddle, or try to be my "friend." She honestly and authentically connected with me since my infancy. We shared a closeness that's hard to explain. When I went away to college, we still spoke on the phone twice a week. One of those conversations would include my father and the other did not. She had the motherly ability to sense by the tone of my voice if something was wrong. She just knew. Reflecting on our relationship, the most important thing she did consistently was to listen. She always made time to listen. She'd drop everything to spend time together. She once equated spending the time we shared to eating a hot fudge sundae. I now realize this is the basis for any enduring relationship. If the other person doesn't feel like they are seen or heard, then there is no true relationship. My mother's dedication to the success of our relationship permeated our family so I wouldn't notice my father's lack of participation. Therefore, only one parent needs to establish that emotional connection for a child to develop a successful sense of self.

My father never shared stories about his childhood with me. My paternal grandparents had passed away by the time I was born. So, the stories I heard were secondhand. I've pieced together a patchwork of stories about how my father was raised, enough to make assumptions and educated guesses about his upbringing.

When my paternal grandmother was five months pregnant with my father, my grandfather owned and operated a liquor store. One night in December, a man entered the store to rob it. My grandfather reached under the counter, presumably for a gun, and was shot and killed. In one minute, many lives were changed. My grandmother was given medicine by her physician "to calm her nerves," without regard to the baby growing inside her uterus. It was 1937. She was single, pregnant, and had three small children at home. Without support from her family, she chose to continue operating the liquor store. When she gave birth to my father four months later, she was working every day to keep everything together. She wasn't able to be emotionally available to her new son. When my father was two years old, my grandmother married a traveling liquor salesman who raised my father as his child. My father's siblings were older and while this new man in their life took care of all of them, my father was his favorite. He indulged him with new bicycles and toys, while the older children got hand-me-downs. The older siblings may have developed resentment toward my father. Since the marriage was still fresh, my grandmother often went out with her new husband, leaving the children to fend for themselves. This was a different era when children were best seen and not heard.

There were fewer family outings and more couple outings. My father's parents exhibited the behaviors listed earlier in this chapter regarding things parents do to encourage and boost narcissism. He was essentially raised by both an emotionally unavailable parent (my grandmother) and a parent who overindulged him to gain his love (her new husband). It was a clear recipe for him to grow into a narcissist.

WHAT HAVE YOU LEARNED?

Narcissists aren't born. They're created through their upbringing. Their emotions never fully develop. Parents shape and form narcissists through years of simultaneously ignoring and overindulging them which qualifies as abuse and/or neglect.

Who influences child development more than parents? They control the environmental factors of child development.

Learning my father was in competition with his daughter was an extremely difficult realization. It shook me deeply and I questioned our entire relationship. Shockingly, six years after that realization, it's been two relatively peaceful years and he's still at it. Recently, I spoke at an awards ceremony at a big amateur golf tournament where I was the general chairman. My father never misses this annual ceremony as he's a past chairman and sits on the dais. This day, he left early. He couldn't stand seeing me at the podium. Once a narcissist, always a narcissist.

In his book *Traumatic Narcissism*, Daniel Shaw discusses the trauma inflicted by a lack of recognition in childhood which lies at the heart of pathological narcissism. He reinforces the notion to understand and appreciate others as subjects in their own right, we each need to have experienced this understanding and appreciation in early childhood. Shaw writes, "to feel seen, understood, cared about, paid attention to, affirmed, supported and lovingly cherished is crucial to development." Without these things, we can't develop a strong, healthy sense of self. Without a strong sense of self, relationships are difficult and painful—in some cases impossible. The lack of a strong sense of self contributes greatly to the formation of narcissism.

The antidote to creating and raising a narcissist is to provide the necessary emotional connection to our children. The importance of establishing a connection resulting in attachment after birth and into childhood can't be understated. Once more, I want to reinforce the fact that narcissists aren't born. They're unfortunately created and nurtured by emotionally unavailable parents who exhibit specific behaviors during their childhood. If you consistently follow the seven positive directives above about what parents can do, you'll improve your chance of raising an emotionally healthy, narcissist-free child. In addition, it's just good parenting advice.

Every parent should be present and praise their children appropriately for actual achievements and teach empathy. This is the greatest gift you can give your child. It's a gift of supporting them in building inner resources which they'll draw on in any conflict or crisis. Parents have a short window of time to build their child a foundation which will prevent them from developing narcissistic traits.

4

THE WRECKING BALL DEMOLITION PLAN

"Sometimes you don't realize how terrible you were
treated until you are explaining it to someone else."

Anonymous

recently realized I grew up with a deep emotional privilege. My mother provided a safe environment while telling me I was smart, pretty and teaching me empathy for others. She created a cozy bubble where I felt comfortable and secure. I grew more self-confident each year. She exposed me to all kinds of people, different races, religions, and backgrounds. I learned empathy because my mother had many different relationships and we talked about everything. Every book she read to me, every show we watched, or movie we saw – we discussed afterward. Just like the character Atticus Finch from Harper Lee's novel *To Kill a Mockingbird* says, "You never really understand a person until you consider things from his point of view ... until you climb into his skin and walk around in it."

Basically, my mother made sure I wasn't a narcissist by creating a foundation of inner resources. What are inner resources? They're defined as having the ability to help yourself manage or achieve something. I grew up thinking of inner resources as the knowledge I am loved. This knowledge provided me with the power to take risks, try new things and make new friends. The opposite of this power is the inability to cope with difficult situations for a person with little or no inner resources.

After the loss of my mother, my father lost his inner resources. He lost the narcissistic supply she provided.

Narcissists come from a place of vulnerability, low self-esteem, and insecurity. The only way for them to thrive or perhaps survive is to find a source of narcissistic supply to feed their ego. The term "narcissistic supply" refers to the praise, admiration, envy, and recognition they need like oxygen. It's as if they have no inner resources to draw upon. My father will actually solicit narcissistic supply if it's not forthcoming.

- ⊚ *"How do I look?"*
- ⊚ *"Did you see what I won?"*
- ⊚ *"How about these things I bought on sale?"*
- ⊚ *"Aren't I the best _____ ?"*

He might even provide evidence to prove his case, social proof, like newspaper clippings, that are hard to refute. There's no choice but to offer the needed narcissistic supply just to move the conversation along to something else.

His actions at this time, after my mother's death, now seem like a desperate scheme to quickly replace his supply and regain his perceived strength. He needed to appear strong to others and was willing to do anything, including hurting me to accomplish it.

Looking back, none of my father's actions in this chapter were shocking. Yet, I was completely unprepared. Generally, daughters aren't super comfortable with their dad dating whether it's after a divorce or a death. Daughters want to believe they come first to their dad. I now recognize this behavior in many men who choose their girlfriend or second wife over their daughter. Sometimes the daughters are adults and sometimes they're teens. I've watched some of our family members do this after a divorce. The daughter is left confused why her father would choose a seemingly random girlfriend over his daughter. She feels lost, maligned, and angry. The daughter didn't cause the divorce or do anything to deserve this treatment. I've also seen this happen to friends of my daughters. In their teens, they become pawns in their father's new relationship. For one girl, she has ended up at 15 with no relationship with her father as he chose his new wife over her. It's sad for both of them. He's the adult yet can't seem to see the forest for the trees. He's completely invested in his new wife and doesn't see the pain and trauma he's causing his only child. He's so desperate for someone to confirm his masculinity and make him feel desired as a man.

I grew up with the confidence some facts are certainties, like our unalienable rights. I believed in G-d and America and that my parents loved me. As a child, I felt guilty for favoring my mother. She was everything – my friend, confidante, advisor, counselor, and mom. I never once doubted my father loved me. I felt he was the same man my mother presented to me. When she died, I had a hard time recognizing him. At first, I thought it was grief, but as time went on, I came to see grief wasn't the problem.

My father believed a year was the appropriate amount of time to grieve the loss of his wife and subsequently began dating. I wasn't a child or even a young adult. I was 40 years old. I understood the whys, I just wasn't ready to move on from grieving my mother yet. I especially wasn't ready for my father to debut his new girlfriend at my largest annual work fundraiser.

I suppose he always needed to publicize his every accomplishment and award. He's the one who taught me how to write a press release. I didn't realize this need would extend to his relationship status.

In Chapter 2, some of the characteristics of a narcissist listed are an exaggerated sense of self-importance as well as a belief one is special and requires excessive admiration. My father wanted people to envy him, not feel sorry for his loss. Similarly, in the multi-awarded television show "Veep," Julia Louis-Dreyfus portrays the Vice-President of the United States, Selina Meyer, who embodies our notion of the politician as a narcissistic self-promoter who believes in nothing except winning power just for the sake of winning. Selina's staffers enable her and fawn over her, providing her with the necessary narcissistic supply. Her behavior is best described as blindly ambitious without regard for anyone who gets in her way or any ethical standards.

It seemed like my father needed to announce his relationship with trumpets, fanfare, and spotlights. He decided there should be an all-out blitz to announce his new status as if he was marketing himself. First, he posted her photo on Facebook for all his connections to see. Then he began planting seeds, telling people in our small community he had big news. Then the big charity gala, my work event, where she'll accompany him just a year after he lost his wife.

My father needed to feel this approval in our small community perhaps to the level of admiration. Remember that philosophical question, "If a tree falls in the forest and no one is there to hear it, did it make a sound?" It's the same for my father. He needs people to witness his actions and validate them. He desperately wanted people to know he was interested in this woman and "dating" her no matter the impact on the family.

Why does he need to issue an all-points bulletin about his dating status? Why such a desperate need to have every move documented for public consumption? He probably would've loved being a reality show star. It would be a dream come true to have cameras following his every move 24/7. It's almost as if life isn't quite happening unless his actions are announced. He apparently needs to report his activities and list all his awards and accolades. I never noticed these peculiarities when my mom was alive. She buffered most of our communication and I had few interactions without her presence.

My father ends up attending my big work event without his friend. The stress of the whole situation plus the regular stress of my job equaled me becoming very ill at the event.

A few days later was Rosh Hashanah, the Jewish New Year. The holiday marks the beginning of ten days of introspection and repentance culminating in the holiday of Yom Kippur, also known as the Day of Atonement. Rosh Hashanah and Yom Kippur are the two High Holy Days in the Jewish religion. For non-Jewish readers, this is our Christmas and Easter, all in ten days. When I was growing up, we gathered as a family for both holidays at different family homes after attending services at the temple. We belonged to the same synagogue since my parents were married. Due to a drop in population in the area – jobs after college and retirement, we had few people left in our congregation. A decision was made to sell the temple, and this would be our last high holy days in the building. Mom's funeral was held there just last year.

On Rosh Hashanah, I sat in the synagogue and mourned my mother. I mourned the last services at our synagogue. I mourned whatever relationship I thought I'd developed with my father over the last year. I cried through the entire service. I didn't speak directly to my father, but he didn't speak to me or my kids, either. He sat next to me, silent. After the service, he asked if we'd like to join him for lunch.

I told him I wasn't feeling well.

He sent me an email later on Rosh Hashanah night inform-
ing me "today you got even with me on our most religious
holiday. You hurt me." His statement was alarmingly obtuse,
he didn't see me at all. Instead of seeing my pain, grief, and
heartache, he made it about him. My father went right into one
of his patented "narc spins." He exhibited highly narcissistic
behavior as he can't express empathy and he needs to make
everything about him.

I spoke with Patricia, a genuinely lovely person, easy to talk
to, and ready to share her story. She grew up with a narcissistic
father, which has impacted her life and her relationships.
Patricia told me her dad felt people were out to get him, but
that's the paranoia with alcoholism and being a narcissist.
Everything had to be his way. If you did something, it was
either against him or for him. If you weren't smiling, you
were mad at him. It wasn't because you didn't feel well, it was
about him. Everything is personal and either a compliment
or an insult.

My misery, grief, and tears were staged purposefully in
the temple to somehow spite my father. Expressing my grief
or just feeling sad in his presence was forbidden. He decided
our place of worship was neither the time nor place to express
these feelings.

In the movie "Mean Girls," Regina George is a classic
narcissist who can't exhibit empathy to her friend Karen
when Karen tells her she can't go out as she's feeling sick.
Regina responds "Boo, you whore." It's always all about the
narcissist and their needs without concern for anyone else,
no matter how close.

In the months after mom died, I tried to wrap my father into our family, our daily activities. I spoke with him every day and invited him to everything, from soccer games to barbeques and birthday parties. Often, he didn't speak or interact, and we chalked it up to grief. I had no idea what grief looked like, so I gave him lots of space. When he was an hour late to our youngest daughter's birthday party, I never asked why. We went as a family to Disney World in November, as we had in previous years. He was terribly unhappy the whole trip, speaking very little. He genuinely hated when he wasn't in charge. He needed to be the leader and disliked when we led the way at the parks. However, we continued blaming his behavior on grief. We didn't speak about the terrible times after the trip. Then we went as a family to Arizona in March. Again, we tried to do things together, but he was uninterested. One evening, the resort had fire pits blazing and we had the makings of s'mores. We were all headed outside. Our kids were nine and five and gleeful with excitement. My father said he was going to watch television instead of spending time with his family. We went out and had fun making ooey-gooey s'mores together by the open fire. It was a sweet memory he opted out of, so he could sit in front of the TV and sulk. I later asked why he didn't want to join us?

He replied, *"I don't like s'mores."* But it was never about the s'mores, it was about the experience of being together and enjoying the kids' excitement. This was enlightening, revealing, and the first time I thought maybe it's not all grief.

Narcissists take any challenge to their behavior as if the criticism is some kind of permission to do worse. Later in

Chapter 11, you will see this play out with my father on our vacation. Similarly, my father didn't appreciate my challenges and resulted in him doubling down on his selfish behavior with little regard for anyone else. If I was going to continue to try to repair our relationship again, blah, blah, blah, was all he heard. He might as well enjoy himself.

The next Sunday we have dinner at his house. I make dinner and clear out more of my mother's drawers. While cleaning, when it's just the two of us, he tells me, *"You'll have to meet her at some point."*

I ask him, *"Are you getting married while you're in Vegas?"*

He replies, *"No."*

I mention, *"You really need a pre-nuptial agreement."*

He says, *"Of course,"* and adds, *"She wants to move here for the summers and live in Florida in the winter."*

After "meeting" on Facebook, they spent a week together during the Fall. Now they're meeting in Vegas and she's talking about moving here. I don't respond. Will she move into my parent's home? Sleep in my mother's bed? I don't know what to say. Did she even know about these plans? Were the feelings reciprocal?

When I mentioned the need for a pre-nuptial agreement, he didn't get angry. It took months for him to react to this statement. He saved up all his anger and released it in a narcissistic rage storm I've shared in Chapter 5.

I interviewed Phoebe, who compensated for the hurt she suffered growing up with a narcissist parent with an acerbic wit and plenty of sarcasm. Phoebe readily shared stories about her narcissist with me. According to Phoebe, her mother needed to be needed. She discovered narcissists can only function with a protective shield. For my father, my mother was his protective shield. It was obvious he was actively looking for a replacement.

Funny, at this point in my journey, I was unfamiliar with the term narcissism. I thought the purpose of my father's words and actions was to hurt me. I was grieving my mother and he kept hurting me. I felt the damage of the wrecking ball on the relationship I thought I had with my father. Now I see he was without his narcissistic supply from my mother, he desperately needed to plug in a substitute supply. He also needed to be portrayed as strong not weak and be envied and admired. He was on a mission, whether conscious or not and my feelings weren't relevant.

WHAT HAVE YOU LEARNED?

After mom's death I discovered my father, and I had no line of communication. She was always the connector, the translator, the peace maker, and the fixer. We had no idea how to resolve conflicts or speak to each other about difficult subjects. I was still trying to repair and retain the relationship. I wanted to continue being his daughter. I still wanted my father in my life. I didn't know he was a narcissist. I was hurt, angry, frustrated and confused. I genuinely wanted to repair our problems and maintain a relationship.

Mom died in 2010, the events I've described above happened the following year. As I look back, I realize it might seem like I was being unfair, holding my father to my mother's standard of caring and kindness. I believe the trauma of her sudden death combined with his peculiar actions caused me to react from my gut which may appear unreasonable. As a reader on the outside looking in, you may look at my father's behaviors and feel this isn't narcissism as defined in Chapter 2. As you continue reading, you'll see the narcissism only becomes more pronounced, I assure you.

On the very rare occasion I will say to my husband, *"Joseph, when you said this ___ , it made me feel like this ___."*

His response is it's never his intention to hurt me. He loves me. He's sorry that he hurt me. The feeling is mutual, and we keep the lines of communication open. We practice the same behaviors with our daughters.

When I said that to my father, he launched into all the things he's doing and how he's grieving my mother. That worked for me in the first year. But then I started questioning why it only seemed to make things worse. It was as if I was catching him in a web of lies. Nothing was as it seemed. Nothing was as I thought. My mother always "resolved" disagreements. She would tell each of us everything was fine, and the other person didn't mean it so let's move on and come to dinner. I was a child and then a teenager. I thought this was normal. I didn't understand you need resolution to have a better relationship. Sometimes you need to have an uncomfortable conversation to better the relationship. You need to trust the other person. I discovered after my mother's death; I didn't trust him.

This doesn't work with everyone. I had a friend in law school I'll call Rachel. I thought she was a good friend throughout the three years. In our last year, I became friends with other classmates. I didn't see it at the time, but this made Rachel upset. She was jealous. Instead of expressing her feelings, she acted out, like a toddler. When I was with these other friends, Rachel would come up and start taking shots at me, for laughs. *"We all know Lynn's so dumb about this subject, right guys?"* she would say.

I was offended, actually livid. I'd never exhibit this behavior toward her. I'd never attempt to embarrass a friend in public, not my style. I decided to let it lie until after the bar exam. I had to compartmentalize my reaction. I couldn't spend time analyzing the relationship and meeting with her to discuss it. I had to study. After the bar, I made a lunch date with Rachel to see her and discuss what happened. Amazingly, she reacted how my father would react in years to come. She got quiet and said little, no response. The energy at the table became uncomfortable. We said our goodbyes and I never heard from her again. I guess it wasn't a relationship worth saving.

When a narcissist hears someone express this to them, they don't hear they hurt someone they love. They hear it as a criticism. They hear it as it's their fault. They don't want to talk about anything that could possibly be their fault.

Once you understand the narcissist, you know nothing is about you. It's always, always about them. Your pain is meaningless. Your success is meaningless unless it competes with them. They're always in competition with everyone else.

THE RUIN OF RAGE STORMS

"But yet thou art my flesh, my blood, my daughter –
Or rather a disease that's in my flesh,
Which I must needs call mine. Thou art a bile,
A plague-sore or embossed carbuncle,
In my corrupted blood. (Act 2, Scene 4,.218-25)

King Lear addresses Goneril (his daughter) with manipulative rage.

Some people compare a narcissist's rage storm to an actual storm like a hurricane. There often is some warning it's coming if you see the signs. Once it hits, all you can do is ride it out until it's over to see how much damage occurs. A narcissistic rage storm can take many forms: sometimes yelling and screaming and sometimes withdrawing into seething silence and passive-aggressive behaviors. The goal of the narcissist is always to hurt the other person as a defense mechanism because they feel injured. Sometimes the passive-aggressive rage storm comes in writing with caustic sarcasm or purposeful neglect. Rage storms often begin when a narc spin goes a little too far. A rage storm is a larger, more destructive narc spin. Remember, the narcissist always reacts to their perceived injury, as a blow to their inflated image.

Well-known examples of rage storms can be found in literature. One example is the play *King Lear* by Shakespeare. Even if you've never read *King Lear*, the story is relatable and relevant. Lear's primary flaw is he values appearances above reality. He wants what narcissists always want, for people around him to pay attention, follow his directions and show respect, especially in public. When he doesn't get what he wants, Lear flies into a rage storm. He's angry when his daughters, Regan and Goneril tell him what to do. Regan has the unmitigated gall to tell Lear he's at fault. He doesn't appreciate Goneril and should apologize. You can almost feel the storm coming on from Lear's reaction. In the above-referenced quote, Lear goes off on Goneril. He calls her a disease. This can happen when narcissists don't get what they want.

The world witnessed a similar narcissistic rage storm when U.S. Vice President Mike Pence followed the U.S. Constitution by certifying the official federal count of Electoral College votes in the 2020 presidential election. President Trump mistakenly believed Vice President Pence had unilateral power to subvert the will of the states, millions of voters, and do as Trump wished. When Pence followed the Constitution, he enraged President Trump. The President went into a narcissistic rage storm at his "Make America Great Again" rally outside the White House, which incited the January 6, 2021 attack on the U.S. Capitol building. Trump needed everyone to know he wouldn't be President again and it was Pence's fault. He turned his rage into actual violence by provoking thousands of protesters to act on his rage.

The Associated Press headlined this, *"Trump's Rage Ignites Mob Assault on Democracy."* This was a narcissistic rage storm of monumental proportions for the whole world to see.

A rage storm can also be expressed in writing. Trump's tweets were little storms of their own, setting off fireworks along the way. On the morning of January 6, 2021, Trump tweeted, "States want to correct their votes, which they now know were based on irregularities and fraud, plus corrupt process never received legislative approval. All Mike Pence must do is send them back to the States. AND WE WIN. Do it, Mike, this is a time for extreme courage!" After the big speech by Trump, he went back to the White House. An hour later, Trump tweeted "Mike Pence didn't have the courage to do what should have been done to protect our country and our Constitution, giving States a chance to certify a corrected set of facts, not the fraudulent or inaccurate ones which they were asked to previously certify. USA demands the truth!" According to multiple reports, President Trump silently sat and watched on television as the insurrection unfolded amid repeated requests from staff, family, and elected officials to intervene and call for an end to the violence. After three hours of chaos, Trump uploaded a video to his Twitter, denouncing the riots but still maintaining the false claim the election was stolen. Ironically, Rolling Stone magazine dubbed this moment, "both Shakespearean and profoundly dangerous," essentially, comparing Trump to King Lear.

What causes narcissists to fly into a rage storm? Mostly it happens when they don't get their way; even in President Trump's case, when it's completely unreasonable.

OTHER MOTIVATIONS CAN INCLUDE WHEN NARCISSISTS:

- *Feel criticized,*
- *Aren't the center of attention,*
- *Are confronted with some wrongdoing,*
- *Ask to be accountable for their actions, or,*
- *VIP status isn't given.*

We know narcissists need their narcissistic supply which keeps feeding their ego. If their supply ceases, this can trigger a narcissistic injury. Other things can also cause a narcissistic injury like neglect, real or perceived, and criticizing the narcissist or challenging them. A narcissistic rage storm is the consequence of this narcissistic injury.

Once a narcissist feels this injury, they go into a blame storm, sometimes one of epic proportion.

This was the point in my journey when I began thinking my father's behavior couldn't just be caused by the grief of losing his wife. My mother was gone more than a year. The words, actions, and conduct of my father were abnormal. I started thinking something else was happening. I began researching mental illness and narcissism. The words in his emails and his actions were completely different.

During this period of time, my father seemed angry all the time. Inviting him over to dinner didn't improve the situation. Asking him to attend my daughter's dance performance didn't change his attitude. Then, after I sent him a concerned email he responded with his own email. He said he didn't feel part of dinner at my home as my in-laws were there too. I spoke with Phoebe about the narcissist in her life, her mother. Phoebe knew as long as you stay on the narcissist's script, you will continue to get their approval. It's when you divert from the script which causes the narcissist to go into a rage storm or withdraw. We definitely were not staying on my father's script like my mother did, providing the necessary narcissistic supply. Every time we have a problem, he turns the tables to position himself as the victim. He immediately reacts saying, *"If you don't want me around, I understand."*

If I said his words or actions hurt, he responded with sweeping generalities as if everything he does is horrible. He was never willing to talk. He wanted things to return to "normal," how they were when my mom was still alive.

Nothing was ever resolved. I swallowed my discomfort and anger to keep the peace.

These actions are typical of narcissists. There's even a term for it – splitting. Splitting is defined by Psychology Today as, "a very common ego defense mechanism." The narcissist splits every issue into good or bad. They deny their negative thoughts or words while accusing others of disapproving. My father exhibits this in the "valentine" you'll read later in this chapter. These events now feel small compared with later rage storms, merely glimpses of things to come.

Phoebe compared her mother's narcissism to having an addiction in that as her child, she didn't know what was coming next. One time, her mother cut herself while peeling potatoes. She was bleeding, and she said to Phoebe *"see what you made me do?"* This made Phoebe become hyperalert and completely in control of her own emotions so that she didn't react to anything.

My father, during this time, was building a Category 4 narcissistic rage storm and I didn't know when it would make landfall.

On Valentine's Day, February 14, I receive this note in a bag left in my front door with candy for my daughters. The storm arrived.

Lynn,

Happy Valentines Day!

I am writing this note to you because I am trying to understand our situation.

It seems if everything I am doing you tell me I am purposely doing to hurt you. You tell me that all I ever did with your husband was hide from him when you went out with him.

You seem to want to stop our relationship because I am only hurting you.

I have thought about this for many weeks. What is clear to me is that you loved your mother and believe she did everything for you + your family.

I also believe that for whatever reason I was never part of that relationship.

I never participated in those times. I only am a negative in what you remember.

Your comments to me about Mom's money — like only she worked — not how we saved together. That it was our savings — that we worked hard for.

you also are consumed about the things in our (my) house, yes, I took down the pictures — but have displayed them differently.

yes I have given you anything you wanted but that doesn't matter to you.

I am the big negative. you have started to leave me — First Thanksgiving vacation — now Spring vacation. I now realize we will never go anyplace again as a family.

I now understand you are only interested in me doing an agreement if I chose someone to live with or marry. So that I protect the things and money for your family.

I have tried to understand. You have met with me 3 times with written notes to tell me how bad I have been. Between my phone and actions, all have done only to hurt you — so not true!

But no more emails — no more phone calls no more dinners — that it has come to this I am sorry, life goes on — I don't know how long I will live but it seems if I can do it alone or with whom ever.

I remember sending boxes of food to Michigan boxes to Boston — driving every day to Rochester

All things I did. I remember the < Award
NCCC + BOCES for Joseph. The UNDER 40's
Awards — all things I did not your mom.
I pushed the vocations not your mom. I
put together the gifts. — She worked for the
insurance monies to help you. I bought the
items I brought to your house not mom.
In fact many of the things we did together
for you + your family we discussed and agreed
upon before doing.

Well it doesn't matter anymore —
do what you want to do ; you have hurt me and
I am going to do whatever I have to —
to maintain my health, live my life and
be me. If you chose to take my grandchildren
away from me also — I understand.
As to you + Joseph I hope you
have everything you want — good health
and prosperity.
I wish the best for Allison
+ Madeline. I love them!

Regards
your father. 2/14/12

I was stunned to receive this furious note disguised as a "valentine." It read like a manifesto of rage and resentment. Years of built-up bitterness for not receiving enough praise, attention, or accolades heaped upon him. It revealed many narcissistic characteristics from Chapter 2. He wrote defensively, furious with any criticism of his actions and exasperated by my challenges. Utilizing more "splitting" in the first few statements, he generalizes all his words and actions hurt me. He expressed outright jealousy when stating he wasn't part of the relationship with my mother and me.

When I asked months ago if he planned to marry, I mentioned the need for a pre-nuptial agreement. He agreed. My mother dutifully put money into her retirement fund, never missing a payment. She died before spending one dollar. In the same discussion, I naively said, *"I'm sure it wasn't my mother's intention to leave her retirement account to a woman instead of her grandchildren."* I wanted to protect my mom's legacy.

Now he attacked me saying, *"Your comments to me about mom's money – like only she worked – not how we saved together. That it was* our *savings that we worked hard for."* This is a sore spot and he's angry. You can almost feel the venom in his letter. Since he didn't have honest conversations with me, I tried to put the clues together: getting the house ready, planning on staying with this woman in Florida for the winter, and then here in the summer. At some point, marriage was the next step. After this valentine, I decided to avoid further discussions about money. Then he continued, *"I now understand you are only interested in me doing an agreement if I choose someone to live with or marry. So that I protect the things and money for your family."*

This is exactly what I wanted, yet I can't fathom why it makes him mad. Yes, I want him to continue his next chapter. However, I don't think it's cool to leave my children's legacy to some woman.

I've challenged him repeatedly by not doing exactly what he wants. He takes these challenges as direct attacks. This is how he responds – taking credit for all the good and none of the bad. As we know from Chapter 2, narcissists require excessive admiration and selfishly take advantage of others to achieve their ends. He wants acknowledgment for sending boxes of food to me at college or "driving every day to Rochester" when I was in a near-fatal car accident at age 18 and in the hospital for three weeks. He wants me to know it was his idea to plan vacations, gifts, and items he brought to my house, not my mom. She can't argue or defend herself. He must be superior to mom even after her death. He takes credit my mother can't dispute from the grave as if I've lost my memory. This rage storm crossed over to a new place.

I spoke with Patricia, who survived the emotional abuse from her narcissistic father. After she could no longer take the constant abuse from him, working for him and the family-owned company, Patricia resigned. A few months after her resignation, on her youngest child's birthday, she received a phone call from her brother. She naively thinks it's to wish her son a happy birthday.

Her brother says, "Hello Patricia, would you please hold on?"

Her dad comes on the phone and while raising his voice exclaims, *"PATRICIA – THIS IS YOUR FATHER SPEAKING. YOU COULD LIVE WITH ME BEFORE I HAD CANCER BUT NOW THAT I HAVE CANCER YOU CAN'T LIVE WITH ME. YOU'VE STUCK IT UP MY ASS. YOU'VE STUCK IT UP YOUR BROTHERS ASS AND YOUR OTHER BROTHERS ASS. YOU'VE STUCK IT UP THE COMPANY'S ASS. HAVE A GOOD LIFE!"* This was her father's rage storm.

I especially like the *"Have a good life!"* at the end. Similar to my father's closing of his toxic valentine: *"I hope you have everything you want ... "* Somehow narcissists manage to be disingenuous in their good wishes.

In Chapter 2, we learned narcissists have trouble handling criticism. In turn, they often have significant interpersonal problems. They easily feel slighted; react with rage or contempt, belittle others to appear superior; have difficulty regulating their emotions; and harbor feelings of insecurity, shame, vulnerability, and humiliation. The St. Valentine's Massacre rage storm demonstrated all of the above.

WHAT HAVE YOU LEARNED?

My father's narcissistic rage storm is like both King Lear and President Trump. They all share a desire to be adored and revered for their achievements. They want people to simply do as they say. They despise being challenged or questioned. How long do rage storms last? They vary in length from narcissist to narcissist. Sometimes it feels like my father's continues non-stop, some smaller, some larger. How do they end? Sometimes they end in scorched earth, like President Trump.

The valentine from my father left me with more questions. I lost my mother and now didn't understand my father. I had a hard time believing he didn't care as if his love ran out. I was trying to keep him in my life, and he was trying to say he didn't want me.

Narcissistic rage storms may appear to come out of the blue but can be predictable if you look for clues. I didn't even know what to call it at the time. I was perplexed why he ranted, disparaging mom's memory and trying to change the past. In retrospect, he left clues; not talking at dinner with my in-laws, taking phone calls at inappropriate times, and arguments when things didn't go his way.

Just like King Lear and former President Donald Trump, the storm brewed when things didn't go their way. Their chaotic, angry energy had to be released. King Lear said horrible things to his daughter. President Trump incited destruction and fatal violence on our U.S. Capitol and inno-cent people. I received a "valentine," wishing me well and saying he understood if I don't want him in my life.

This was more "splitting," attempting to make events appear black or white. I'm responsible for the future of our relationship. I just wanted him to act like my father or the person I thought he was.

TOXIC BOSSES CAUSE CHAOS

"Narcissistic bosses are bullies in the workplace. They target you if you don't kiss up to them and always agree with them. They hate people that work creatively and come up with new ideas because they can't."

Anonymous

ow does a narcissist present themselves at work? Narcissists often manifest as toxic leaders in the work culture. They exhibit the same characteristics listed in Chapter 2 with subtle differences. Narcissists as toxic bosses demonstrate specific characteristics intended to make employees miserable. They need everyone to be on edge all the time, uncomfortable in their position, with little job security. Toxic bosses pride themselves on their omnipotence and reign of terror. They're inconsistent, incapable of giving positive reinforcement, and incorrigible. I actually worked for three of these toxic bosses and the fourth is from a movie.

- *Miranda the Merciless Maven (from "The Devil Wears Prada")*
- *Jeff the Jovial Jerk*
- *Chris the Calculating Commander*
- *Don the Demanding Dictator*

One of the best examples of a narcissistic boss on the big screen can be seen in the 2006 movie "The Devil Wears Prada." The character Miranda Priestly, played brilliantly by Oscar® winning actress Meryl Streep, portrays the Editor-in-Chief of a fictitious fashion magazine, Runway. Miranda is demanding, ruthless and expects her `every demand to be met.

"Is there some reason that my coffee isn't here? Has she died or something?" This quote personifies Miranda Priestly and conveys her lack of empathy and feelings for others. She expects her staff to perform their assigned tasks, even if it's only getting coffee, and do it well. She is suggesting death is the only possible reason why someone wouldn't have her coffee perfect and ready on time. Her words are delivered with a lack of emotion, demonstrating Miranda's absence of emotion and how little she cares about her employees. Miranda doesn't invest in her employees as they leave often. She only cares if they do their job, if not she'll merely hire a replacement.

Miranda the Merciless Maven meets all the characteristics of a toxic boss. She expects employees to be on call 24 hours a day and respond instantly no matter the day or time. She knows people are replaceable and never invests in them, as she's aware they'll only stay for a short while. As a narcissist, she uses people for her benefit and discards them when they no longer have any value to her.

While narcissists in the office check all the boxes of traditional narcissists defined in Chapter 2, they also demonstrate definitive attributes shared amongst their tribe. Each toxic boss has an individual style of leading a group or organization, however, there are ten hallmarks of a narcissist in the workplace.

1. They don't take responsibility for their poor decisions

Narcissists are the first ones to smile for the TV cameras when things go right but rarely take responsibility when things go wrong. These toxic bosses are known for throwing people under the bus, perhaps even while driving the bus. Of course, I say this facetiously, many people have experienced these feelings. In one case, a boss easily accepted voluntary assistance for a very technical computer scheduling project working with government resources from a loyal employee who doesn't possess the necessary skills to complete the task. The boss accepts his offer, so he doesn't have to find someone else to do the task. The employee desperately wants to succeed but ends up creating even more problems. Once it went south, the toxic boss takes the task away from the employee and blames him for the problem instead of taking responsibility as the chief. This subsequently leads to enough reasons for the toxic boss to have the employee escorted out by Human Resources (HR). The toxic boss doesn't like uncomfortable conversations or conflict. The employee was loyal to the organization for over 18 years yet received no respect from the toxic boss. Good leaders take credit for both the bad and the good, that's part of the job.

2. They avoid conflict at all costs - they love consensus and hate disagreement.

Toxic bosses don't want to have uncomfortable conversations, ever. They make edicts and you either abide or leave. I once worked for a CEO, Jeff who believed he was the ultimate leader and completely irreplaceable. The Board of Directors mandated a succession plan Jeff successfully derailed for years until he couldn't push it off any longer. As part of the plan, they hired me. Jeff welcomed me and introduced me to others. However, he never wanted to have conversations with me. He didn't want to meet with me, period. Jeff was very congenial with a big, boisterous laugh. He loved having special lunches and parties with his staff. He just refused to have a conversation about the work with me.

3. They micromanage EVERYONE.

Narcissists ask you to do a task then email you to check. Then they ask again. Then they ask the person you were supposed to ask. Rinse and repeat. They don't trust anyone, so they never empower or truly delegate authority. It must be exhausting.

Don was hired although he had no nonprofit or fundraising experience. He invited himself to a meeting I was having with a donor. My job was to assist donors in planning their legacy with signed agreements and funding sources. That day I was meeting with a recent widow who was tentative as financial decisions were always made with her husband. I knew she needed patience and I needed to listen reflectively to her wants and desires.

Don barged in on the meeting by interrupting my greeting and stating, *"Lynn, good you're taking notes today. Email those after you type them up and send them to Rose and me."* With one command he established himself as in control, belittling me. It also made clear that Don and I weren't on the same team.

I asked Rose several pointed questions and listened attentively to her answers. She felt a connection to one organization due to her husband and wanted her children notified, but not directly involved.

Don launched into his cookie-cutter proposal he'd just given another donor about a complex endowment fund which would make annual grants to specific areas. Her children would serve on a committee, review the grant applications, and decide where funds should go.

I looked at Don blankly. He was a narcissist. He didn't listen to Rose at all. Instead, he was focused on elevating himself and convincing the board they made the right decision hiring him. He was trying to sound like he knew what he was talking about. I proposed exactly what she wanted, an endowment fund with enough annual interest income to benefit the specific organization she talked about, notifying her designated son. Rose audibly sighed as she was relieved there was another choice after Don's kneejerk proposal. I told her I'd send her the agreements to sign at her convenience. She was appreciative and left.

Don looked at me and said, *"I think that went well, don't you?"* Don didn't know how to read the room. Don micromanaged the entire staff in his own toxic way.

4. They don't communicate well or sometimes even at all

A toxic boss will say something one day and have a completely different way to do the same task the next day. They change their mind quickly. *"I told you to do it this way. Well, no, now I want you to do it that way.*" Sometimes they can't see an analysis if it wasn't their idea. They only understand their own analysis.

During my career, I've been part of different committees that reviewed job candidates for financial investing and accounting. I've seen many presentations and reviewed them by committee. I've witnessed memorable presentations and some less than memorable. Soon after Don began, requests for proposals for our accounting work were sent out. After sitting through three presentations, it was abundantly clear which firm stood out. One firm brought four people to present. They were each expert in their areas. One was the clear spokesperson, but each had a role to play in the presentation. They worked well together as a team and offered that camaraderie as a benefit to any organization. After all the prospective accounting firms departed, our committee discussed the presentations. It was obvious this one firm outshined the competition. The committee readily agreed this firm was our clear choice.

Days after this committee meeting and decision, I shared the story with Don, even though he was present at the interviews. My purpose was to show him what a great team looks like. I genuinely wanted to present a united front to the board and our donors. I told Don this was the team I felt we should emulate. After I explained my case, he responded he didn't see that in the accounting firm's presentation at all. He told me he didn't see the teamwork I described. I was speechless. What do you say? How do you move forward? Of course, he didn't want to be a team. As a narcissist, Don wanted and needed to be the star.

5. **They assume everyone is on call 24/7 no matter their pay or level of responsibility. They have no boundaries (texting/emailing at all hours and days and upset when there's no response)**

Toxic bosses disrespect the personal time of all their employees. Most employees hired into an organization are there for a full-time job during business hours, 40 hours a week. What happens when a toxic boss has an idea in the evening or on the weekend? They email, text, or call their employee. Most of these communications could wait until the next weekday or Monday to discuss it. The toxic boss wants an immediate reply. Most people would make themselves a note or send themselves an email to remember for Monday morning, but not a toxic boss. Their ideas are the most important and require immediate attention and validation.

In the earlier referenced movie, "The Devil Wears Prada," Miranda Priestly is a toxic boss. She expects her assistant to be available any hour of the day and calls her throughout the evening and on weekends. By the end of the movie, Andy, her assistant, played by Ann Hathaway, dramatically throws her cell phone into a Parisian fountain as an abrupt way of resigning from her servitude.

6. They do not plan, they just react

There is no known overall strategic plan for the organization. They constantly lead the organization into new pivots. If this doesn't work, they blame someone or something and pivot again.

Jeff was removed from his position by the Board of Directors due to multiple improprieties. After three months, the Director of Finance rang the emergency alarm and notified the board she couldn't continue as the workload and pressure heaped on her were a genuine threat to her health. They responded quickly with a job posting online with multiple replies.

Out of the blue, the Treasurer of the Board of Directors, Don, who held this responsibility while Jeff executed his improprieties and had signed off on all the financial reporting, which included all the improprieties, volunteered to be the paid CFO. He told the rest of the board, *I want to throw my hat in the ring.*

The Board Chairman replied, *"You're hired."* This major decision was performed without due process or normal operating procedures. Other job candidates weren't considered. The applicant wasn't vetted and there was no background investigation. Nothing that should have happened was done. Most importantly, there was no plan. Don was made Chief Financial Officer by four men who served as Executive Committee members of the governing board of the organization along with him. He had no experience in foundations or nonprofit management. Questions were posed by stakeholders like, *"isn't this like putting the fox in charge of the henhouse?"* This was incredibly bad optics and there was no strategic plan for the organization.

7. They focus on short-term optics without concern for actual solutions or attacking the root cause of the problem

Jeff was the leader of his organization for over 30 years. People revered and respected him. However, there were always those who challenged his techniques and modernization. Jeff listened to several colleagues who told him about a new organization leading the way in modern legacy planning. Their CEO had just published a book about generational wealth, and everyone was talking about the organization. With no strategic plan, input from the Board of Directors, or anyone else's opinion, Jeff engaged the organization to consult for his organization. He didn't care if there wasn't a plan. He needed short-term optics for people to see he was progressive and modern. He even purchased 100 books from their CEO to hand out to donors, sight unseen and book unread. He invited this organization to present to the community at the worst possible opportunity. The consultant they sent was highly qualified. However, the event was an annual meeting which took place in the wrong venue for her presentation. It wasn't about the presentation; it was about Jeff's desperation to remain relevant.

8. They completely ignore turnovers

Narcissists don't want to rehash why someone leaves as it may reflect poorly on them. They choose not to investigate and often demonize outgoing employees as disloyal or not a good fit. Chris the Calculating Commander once said, "*I'm not in the business of begging people to stay.*" The organization had a turnover rate of almost 25 percent in one year. People left because it was such a toxic organization. No one felt they had a modicum of job security. The negative environment helped spread mistrust and a lack of teamwork. Their motto should have been, "We don't invest in our people as they're replaceable." Chris liked pretending he was unaware of such problems.

When an employee received an offer from another organization for more money, a better title, a better opportunity, they'd often go to Chris and tell him. They would say they have an opportunity, but they still love it here. If they were offered a raise, often they would stay. Chris was known for simply wishing people well. He never asked anyone to stay.

9. They are opinionated but without any positive reinforcement - quick to offer criticism but never any coaching.

Narcissists at work will happily shoot down ideas providing no guidance on coming up with better ones. When we receive praise, we usually work harder. We get inspired which creates motivation. When the opposite occurs, most people think, why bother?

At one organization, I had a large annual goal to meet. When world events changed how we do business, many obstacles stood in the way of my goal. Somehow, between the two waves, I met with a record number of prospects and achieved 85 percent of my goal. An impressive achievement during such a crazy time.

I met with Chris, and he said, *"But you didn't achieve your goal."* He never gave one word of positive reinforcement. Perhaps if he'd said, *"While you didn't achieve your goal, your results are impressive. I know we'll continue doing great things together and build this foundation."* Nope, he gave zero.

Don't underestimate the power of praise and positive reinforcement. The lack of it changed my trajectory. I found it hard to give the 110 percent I previously gave. It didn't seem to matter. I continued doing my job in a perfunctory way. I wasn't insubordinate, but I only did what was required. Sadly, I discovered this wasn't sustainable for the long term.

10. They show complete disregard and disrespect for other's time

Jeff was highly credentialed and experienced, and people treated him with great respect. He was accessible and would meet with anyone who requested a meeting. Jeff knew his business well and could be a little intimidating to average people. However, Jeff missed out on a great deal as he did all the talking all the time. He was usually late for meetings. So, people left waiting often assumed he had somewhere better to be. He usually began meetings by speaking about something irrelevant. Perhaps something he heard on the news, the latest gossip in the community, or something from a previous meeting. This had an awkward, off-putting effect on the person with whom he was meeting. Jeff would finally ask them about the day's topic.

This was their one chance to speak. After they expressed their concern, Jeff used all the oxygen in the room, talking endlessly. The other person would just listen to him drone on about something unrelated to their request. Often, nothing was accomplished at these meetings and no further

action was requested. He didn't care about others'
time as only his mattered. He was always the most
important person in the room.

In my research to understand how narcissists exist in the
workplace and how to handle them when it's a problem, I
spoke with Cindy who has two decades of experience working
in Human Resources (HR) for a university. Cindy shared a
story about a narcissist in a department where other employees were having trouble as a result of this person. She had to
help all of them find a way to peacefully co-exist as members
of the same organization.

Narcissists don't usually understand the impact they have
on others, as they are very self-unaware. Narcissists can absolutely wreak havoc on an office or organization. Narcissists
need a "come to Jesus" conversation, a kind of intervention.

Cindy staged an intervention, historically developed to
confront people with substance abuse issues, as this works
for narcissists too. The narcissist and the affected co-workers gather to discuss how they feel as a consequence of the
narcissist's actions. In Cindy's experience, conflict resolution
will only come if you get them all in a room, side by side.
Narcissists have an underdeveloped sense of empathy and
don't form relationships easily as discussed in Chapter 2.
They need to practice reflective listening and learn to build
relationships proactively.

Narcissists need to work on managing their emotions and
their anger. They feel everyone else is stupid. Once people
accept, they're flawed just like everyone else, then a narcissist
can become less defensive. We all have flaws and strengths.

When narcissists finally understand they're doing things in a way that most people find offensive, they may realize they have to fix their behavior. This intervention may help them understand how they impact others.

A new study from the University at Buffalo School of Management showed that narcissists can significantly damage workplace team performance. In this study, researchers define narcissism as a "grandiose sense of self-importance" combined with a lack of empathy for other people—characteristics that can fuel negativity on the job just as defined in Chapter 2. "Narcissists prevent good things from happening," said lead author Emily Grijalva, Assistant Professor of Organization and Human Resources at the University of Buffalo. "Over time, lower levels of narcissism result in teams being able to fully capitalize on the benefits of getting to know each other."

Leadership guru Simon Sinek posits [that the U.S.] "Navy SEALs will never [accept] the toxic person regardless of how athletic they are, how brave, how productive, because the overall health of the team is destroyed as long as they exist."

IF YOU STAY, HOW DO YOU COPE?

If you can leave this toxic employment relationship, you should do it for your own sake. So, if you're in a position where you can find another place to work, go. Cut and run. However, leaving the company may not be an option. If that's the case for you, it is important to develop some coping mechanisms to limit the effects on your mental well-being.

IF YOU STAY, YOU'LL NEED TO:

1. Change your perspective. Accept the fact we cannot change other people; however, we can change ourselves. Mahatma Gandhi said "If we could change ourselves, the tendencies in the world would also change. As a man changes his own nature, so does the attitude of the world change towards him." Show your high level of emotional intelligence by being the change you want to see in the organization. Become empowered by the knowledge your toxic boss's bad behavior is rooted in deep insecurity and change your perspective. Do your best not to take their words and actions personally. When a boss micromanages you, focus on the task. If you choose to stay, then you do the job to the best of your ability, no matter what. Finally, try to avoid interactions with them as much as possible without sounding an alarm. This allows you to focus on doing a good job and you may find them more tolerable if you see and interact with them less.

2. Alter your approach. Accept that each toxic, narcissistic boss has their own communication style. Stop trying to challenge it. Embrace it. The more you learn about their communication preference, the better you'll

be able to adapt and have more effective, efficient conversations. When a boss texts and emails in the evening or on weekends, establish boundaries. Answer them at an appropriate time. Determine your limits. You can't control other people, but you can control whether you react or respond to them. Choose how you'll respond. Keep the relationship strictly professional. Respond in a respectful, positive, professional manner.

3. You can't always get what you want, but you might discover you can get what you need. Be strong enough to know you may not receive the credit you deserve or the positive praise for your exceptional work with this type of leader. Develop the strong inner resources essential to continue. Be confident in yourself and know it doesn't always matter if your boss takes all the credit for your job or doesn't give you one iota of praise. Focus on helping the organization. Toxic bosses don't want to hear the negatives. Put your attention on what you can contribute that's positive. This will help build trust with your boss. Help your boss succeed by becoming a trusted partner. If toxic bosses operate from feelings of fear and demonstrate poor communication skills, help them. Show them you can be trusted to focus on positive tasks for the organization.

WHAT HAVE YOU LEARNED?

Narcissists in the office make toxic bosses. Toxic bosses demonstrate one or more of the ten hallmark characteristics. The movie "The Devil Wears Prada" revealed many of those characteristics onscreen. Toxic bosses come in all shapes and sizes. The toxic bosses described in this chapter – including Miranda the Merciless Maven, Jeff the Jovial Jerk, Don the Demanding Dictator, and Chris the Calculating Commander are different individuals who approach their leadership in different ways. Jeff loved being recognized in public places and called by his name in private clubs. This made everyone aware, Jeff was the most important person in the room. Chris avoided social situations like the plague. He had no interest in belonging to a private club and didn't enjoy going to them. He didn't want to be recognized. He was completely awkward in social situations. Don was always the smartest person in the room and wanted everyone to know it. He was a combination of Jeff and Chris, appreciating being recognized but still socially awkward. Miranda needed to make public appearances, be adored by many, and leave them wanting more. She didn't need to socialize or care about others. All four narcissist bosses in this chapter didn't trust anyone and found it difficult to delegate authority. They didn't empower workers to be independent and micromanaged the work they assigned.

"The smarter you become about your narcissistic boss, the less power your boss will have."

Inc.

COVERT NARCISSISTS WREAK QUIET HAVOC

*"Don't get upset over nothing. I had
no idea this would hurt you.
You're lucky I'm so kind and patient with you."*

Said by Covert Narcissists frequently

WHAT IS COVERT NARCISSISM?

In the 2005 movie "Monster-in-Law," the character Viola, played by Oscar® winning actress Jane Fonda, receives shocking news of her son's sudden engagement. Her son introduces his new fiancé, Charlie, played by Jennifer Lopez, to his mother. Viola immediately sets her sights on orchestrating their break-up. She hosts an extravagant surprise engagement party to make it abundantly clear to Charlie how out of place she'll be in her and her son's upscale world. Viola instructs her son and his fiancé to attend a "barbeque" at her elegant home. Upon arrival, they find everyone dressed in black-tie and formalwear.

Viola tells Charlie there's a new dress waiting for her upstairs along with her son's tuxedo. While Charlie finds a couture gown two sizes too small, Viola sends her son's ex-girlfriend to his former bedroom to visit. Of course, Charlie walks in on the ex-girlfriend kissing her new fiancé!

Charlie finally arrives at the conclusion Viola wants. She exclaims this isn't my world. However, her fiancé tells her she's his world and they leave the party. Most covert narcissists don't go to this level of manipulation as the Hollywood-created Viola to achieve their twisted aims.

Covert narcissism is less obvious and subtler than other forms of narcissism. It's often referred to as shy or closet narcissism. The term "covert narcissism" isn't even listed in the DSM-V (Diagnostic and Statistical Manual of Mental Disorders, 5th version) as is the traditional form of narcissism defined in Chapter 2. This covert type of narcissism shares some characteristics with the narcissism I've discussed throughout this book but has some slight differences. People who possess covert narcissism still feel superior to others, still need admiration and still need to receive special treatment. They simply don't display that outward grandiosity we've come to know and recognize in traditional narcissists.

Covert narcissists typically still like to receive recognition, they like to be acknowledged for their work and their skills, but they behave in passive-aggressive ways. The most on-brand behavior that all covert narcissists share is their passive-aggressive behavior. According to the Mayo Clinic, passive-aggressive behavior is defined as "a pattern of indirectly expressing negative feelings instead of openly addressing them. There's a disconnect between what a passive-aggressive person says and what he or she does." These individuals need to manipulate situations, so they emerge as the helper, the savior, the one who solves the problem and saves the day.

I interviewed three people who've had colorful experiences with the covert narcissist in their life. They're often seen as vulnerable, innocent, and sometimes as a pretender. Throughout this book, I've analyzed many different behaviors and traits of traditional narcissists. What are some benchmark behaviors of covert narcissists to look for?

THEY ARE:

1. Passive-aggressive words and actions

2. Lacking charisma or charm

3. Dismissive toward others

4. Chronic malcontents

5. Manipulative and hypersensitive

6. Highly judgmental

7. Smug or possess a quiet superiority

8. Envious or they possess a sense of entitlement toward what others have

9. Not empathic and don't understand the emotions or pain of others

10. Likely to step in and help out of a desire for recognition

According to clinical psychologist, Dr. Ramani Durvasula, covert narcissists feel like victimized, vulnerable, less skilled narcissists. "They have a lot of contempt, contempt for why they're being held to the same standards as everyone else." Like traditional narcissists, their behavior is a manifestation of their deep insecurities.

In a family relationship, a parent who is a covert narcissist provides the type of abuse you never see coming. It's both shocking and disturbing because you've never seen the person in this role. You wouldn't expect it from this person because they don't necessarily act like a typical narcissist demanding the spotlight. This person looks for recognition but not the same way as a chest-thumping traditional narcissist. This type of person thrives on the chaos of other people. They enjoy the drama.

THEY USE THE SAME EMOTIONALLY ABUSIVE TACTICS AS TRADITIONAL NARCISSISTS:

1. Silent Treatment
2. Triangulation
3. Gaslighting

Covert narcissist parents also use psychological cues to control people such as guilt and shame. A relationship will appear to be close, but in reality, there is a serious lack of boundaries.

Kim, a wife, and mother of four children who works outside the home, makes sure each child participates in sports and activities. Kim told me she's struggled with a mother-in-law who behaves like a covert narcissist. She shared a story with me where her mother-in-law employed the tactic of triangulation. After a year and a half, during which the mother-in-law/grandmother (Anne) gave Kim's family the Silent Treatment, Anne reached out to Barb, Kim's youngest daughter. This seemed strange as Kim has four children and Anne only texted Barb. The text said, "I'm going to ask your dad if you can come over to my house one day."

The eleven-year-old Barb responded with, "*Okay.*"

Anne then texted her son, Barb's dad, to ask if she can pick up her granddaughter Barb one day to come to her house.

Barb's dad texts back, "*I'm sure all the kids would like to see you (Anne). Why don't you come to our house, and you can spend time with all of them?*"

Anne doesn't respond. Later, Anne sends Barb a text saying, "*I asked your dad if you could come over and he said no. I hope to see you soon and please remember how much I love you.*" This is a classic triangulation strategy where the narcissist tells one person something and tells another person something completely different. The goal is to plant seeds of disharmony, creating a wedge between people, often family members. Eventually, they isolate and even pit two people against each other. This tactic allows the narcissist to always be the savior – the peacemaker. It's as if they need to create drama just so they can mediate it and be the pacifier.

According to a Psychology Today article, parents who are covert narcissists master the microaggression. "Unlike the overt narcissist's obvious one-upmanship, the covert narcissist parent uses microaggressions cloaked as oversights, slips of the tongue, humor, help, or caring concern. For a child treated to such abuse, it's death by a thousand cuts."

WHAT ARE TYPICAL SITUATIONS WHERE COVERT NARCISSISTS ENGAGE IN DRAMA?

1. They play the innocent victim. When a covert narcissist parent assumes the role of victim, the parent pivots away from responsibility and blame while soliciting sympathy for all the ways other people, especially their children, disappoint, neglect, and harm them. Parents who act the victim often use guilt and shame to collect attention from their children and others.

   I interviewed Ramona, who's been married for 35 years and now has a tolerable relationship with her mother-in-law. But she remembers a time when it wasn't so. Early on, when Ramona was dating her husband, she'd only met his parents a few times as they lived in different states. They visited over the holidays and there was always a gift exchange. The first year, his parents gave her a lovely, thoughtful gift. The second year, they gave her something similar. The third year, they gave Ramona a generic, white scarf. Ramona was confused by this gift as it was different from the previous ones. Her then-boyfriend asked his mother why she gave her this gift.

The mother replied, *"We just don't seem as close to Ramona."* This "lesser gift" was an attempt to undermine the son's relationship through manipulation. It didn't work as the son easily saw through it when the parent played the victim.

2. As long as you make them look good, they won't object. Your purpose is to make the covert narcissist look good and not embarrass them.

Kim told me about a time when her mother-in-law, Anne, accused her of trying to embarrass her. One day, the whole family was at one of the children's baseball games. Anne asked Kim if she could buy doughnuts for each of the four kids.

Kim calmly replied, *"No, please don't. They've already eaten, and donuts are empty calories."* Kim merely asked Anne not to buy doughnuts. She didn't raise her voice or react other than to simply respond with a polite no.

Later when Anne retold the story to Kim's husband (Anne's son) she didn't hesitate to tell him how upset and mean Kim was to her, and how Kim embarrassed her in front of people. Then, in a complete fabrication, she told her son how Kim dramatically put her arm out to protect the children from their grandmother and screamed, *"NOOOOOO DOUGHNUTS!!"* like in a cartoon. This is a classic example of gaslighting. A narcissist changes the retelling of past events to suit her purposes and make herself the victim. More on gaslighting in Chapter 9.

Kim told me another story when Anne attempted to make her daughter-in-law look bad in the eyes of her own children. At Kim's eldest daughter's play, Anne was invited. She came along with one of their aunts (who was also unkind to Kim). Before the play, Kim was speaking with the aunt while Anne eavesdropped. Kim was making friendly conversation, talking about the various kids' sports and other activities.

Anne called the youngest granddaughter down to ask her a question. Kim heard her say to the little girl, *"I would've come to some of your hockey games, but your mom never told me when you were playing so I couldn't come."*

Kim later reassured her daughter this never occurred. The grandmother always had all the children's sports schedules. Anne consistently twisted things to make herself the victim while throwing Kim under the bus.

3. They don't respect boundaries in your personal life. Everything and anything is their business. Requests for information feel more like a demand rather than a respectful exchange. If you try to set healthy boundaries, it's perceived as pushing back.

Sonia always had religious differences with her mother-in-law. While she's happily married, her mother-in-law has made several attempts, some successful, to indoctrinate her religion on Sonia and her children. Sonia told me in our interview she and her husband haven't declared themselves atheists, but they don't practice any formal religion. Sonia's mother-in-law is a very devout Catholic. When Sonia's first child was born, she and her husband shared their religious views with the mother-in-law. They were very clear in their wishes and their plans for the child.

One day, the mother-in-law invited the young family to come to hear her sing in the choir in church on Sunday. Before Mass began, the mother-in-law carried the child, purportedly to show the baby to her friends. Instead, she took her to the holy water where she began hurriedly sprinkling it on the baby. This was all about the mother-in-law's need to have her grandchild baptized whether it was with or without the parents' permission. Sonia and her husband felt like they were manipulated and disrespected by the mother-in-law.

To illustrate the covert narcissist's lack of boundaries and respect, Sonia shared with me another story about her aunt and uncle. Sonia's uncle was known far and wide for his distaste regarding the Catholic church. He simply didn't believe and didn't attend church. However, his wife was deeply devoted to her faith. Shortly before the uncle's death, he expressed his wishes for a nondenominational memorial service in a park. His wife, Sonia's aunt, decided she wanted a full-on Catholic Mass funeral in the church. It was more important to Sonia's aunt that she got the Mass she wanted rather than respect the wishes of her husband.

4. Creating confusion and passive self-importance. Covert narcissists love to create confusion as a way of maintaining control and passive self-importance. The covert narcissist needs to be the puppet master and only he/she maintains control.

Ramona shared some additional insights with me about her mother-in-law. While they tolerate each other now, her mother-in-law still enjoys creating a cacophony of chaos around family get-togethers. No one knows when relatives are arriving from out of town, where people are staying, or when they will return home. No one knows when the family is getting together or what events are planned. Everything is controlled by the mother-in-law. Only the mother-in-law is privy to this information, and she doesn't share it until it's absolutely necessary. This makes her the matriarch who's put herself in a position of being more important than anyone else. This ensures her presence at every event. There is a lot of dissension in this family. Most of the siblings and cousins don't like one another. The mother-in-law loves when they get together, regardless of whether they have meaningful relationships or not. She seems blithely unaware that the rest of the family doesn't enjoy each other's company. She doesn't care if the family falls apart after she's gone. In the moment, it's paramount for the mother-in-law to convene and have everyone rave about her cooking and baking. The mother-in-law insists upon maintaining control throughout.

5. Your life takes a back seat to the covert narcissist's needs. When something is happening in your life and you're unable to drop everything and immediately attend to the covert narcissist, they quickly become resentful and hurt.

Kim shared an experience with me when her mother-in-law, Anne, lashed out because she didn't receive the attention, she finds so essential. Typically, when Anne visits their house, Kim prepares something special for dinner. On one day, the family had to make a stop which took longer than anticipated. Kim called Anne to see if she was still planning to come over.

She replied, *"Yes."*

So, Kim said, *"Well I guess you can come, you're just going to have to have hot dogs with the kids for lunch."*

With indignation, Anne replied, *"Well, I'm not going to come over because you don't want me to come over."*

The husband told his mother to please come for a visit.

Anne replied, *"She (Kim) doesn't want me to come over so I'm not coming over."* Now she's playing the petulant child to attract attention.

Then the kids were on the phone telling their grandmother to come over.

Anne took this opportunity to tell her grandchildren she wasn't coming over because their mother didn't want her to come.

At that point, Kim sent her mother-in-law a text and apologized for her terse invitation.

Anne replied by text, *"ok."* She went on to tell her son how his wife does and says mean things to her which he doesn't see. This is another attempt at manipulation, perhaps triangulation to prove her needs are most important.

HOW DO THESE PEOPLE MAKE YOU FEEL?

Curious, I asked Kim how she felt when her mother-in-law went into a narcissistic rage storm. She told me she felt annoyed and furious. She said her life is much easier when the mother-in-law keeps her distance. When she does send a text message, Kim's stomach gets upset and she feels rage towards her. Kim stated, *"I find it bizarre after a year and a half that she wants to come to our house. We've invited her three separate times to come and visit over the last year and a half. What's changed?"* Her mother-in-law's actions make her physically sick. *"I'm dreading it. I don't want to see her. I feel like a better person when she's not around."*

I asked the question because I have a physical, visceral response when my father initiates communication. Sometimes it's just an upset stomach. At other times it's irritability or even swollen eyes. My whole body tenses up when I see a text message, a voicemail, or an email from him. The stress he causes is real. My father only calls when he wants or needs something. It's never to ask how I am or how the kids are. It's hard to find things to talk about with him because he doesn't care about discussing subjects that don't revolve around him.

We know from Chapter 2 that 80% of all narcissists are men. We don't know if the 20% of narcissists that are women are specifically covert narcissists although anecdotally, it looks like it. Studies have been done regarding gender and narcissism concluding more men are narcissists than women but nothing specific to covert narcissism.

HOW DO YOU DEAL WITH THESE PEOPLE?

After interviewing Kim, Ramona, and Sonia, I suspect there are many more covert narcissists woven into the fabric of our families than we first believed. What should you do when you encounter this type of person? The coping techniques are like dealing with traditional narcissists as discussed in other chapters.

IT'S ADVISABLE TO:

1. Speak with others. Corroborate your opinions and discuss what you've experienced with other people who've witnessed the narcissist's behavior. This is also a great opportunity to get support from your network.

2. Get familiar with Narcissism (Chapter 2) – both the signs and by reading the stories of others. You may find great comfort in other people's similar experiences and discover you're not alone.

3. It's important to set boundaries and expectations. You must understand narcissists don't change. Instead, change your perspective and your approach to maintain a relationship with this person. When you expect less, you'll either get it or you may be pleasantly surprised. The more you establish boundaries, the more a narcissist will push back and get upset. When you set boundaries, you send a clear message: they are no longer in control.

4. As a last resort, you may have to walk away and end the relationship. Your peace of mind is priceless.

An article, on *pyschcentral.com*, summarized the experience of having a covert narcissist as a mother and their subtle, manipulative ways. "These are the moves of the *covert* narcissistic mother, not the blowhard bluster of the narcissistic man. Still, they are every bit as destructive to her daughter as the overt narcissistic mother, just harder to spot. I would argue the damage is worse because of the insidious nature of the wounds. Like a nick from an extra sharp razor, you don't know you've been cut until you see the blood running down your leg."

WHAT HAVE YOU LEARNED?

Similar to their traditional narcissist counterparts, covert narcissists are emotionally fragile, sensitive, don't handle criticism well, have an outward sense of inferiority, are secretly envious and self-absorbed. The glaring difference is the covert narcissist's trademark is his or her passive-aggressive behavior. Covert narcissists enjoy manipulating your empathy.

By the way, just because they're called covert narcissists doesn't mean they're sneaky or devious. They're just not as overt or extraverted as their narcissist counterparts. They don't blatantly advertise their inflated egos. It's like the surprise in the Cracker Jack box for you to discover. Lucky you!

With both traditional and covert narcissists – everything is always a show. They're always on stage. If they're generous, it's all for recognition. If you need something, unless it fits in with their terms or wants, don't expect to receive it. They only do things to benefit themselves.

When my husband Joseph practiced family law, he would say, *"You can't force someone to be a parent. The court can't make someone be present in their child's life."* I believe this is also true of narcissists. You can't force anyone to be a good grandparent either.

UNSTABLE DESTRUCTION: WHEN YOUR SIBLING IS A NARCISSIST

"Siblings that say they never fight are
most definitely hiding something."

Lemony Snicket

My aunt, on my father's side, once told me a story about her wedding day. She was getting ready in her home and her brother, two years older than her, wouldn't let her in the bathroom. On her wedding day! The entire family were narcissists. This brother was in his twenties then, exhibiting the benchmark manipulative, controlling, selfish behavior of a true narcissist. Narcissists don't always present their standard characteristics and traits in childhood. Sometimes they wait until they're adults to show their true colors.

Narcissist siblings make holidays and family get-togethers miserable. As a result, after the parents have passed away, most siblings no longer spend holidays together. The non-narcissist siblings stay away to remove themselves from the situation, living a life of peace without their narcissist sibling.

Throughout history, we've seen plenty of famous sibling rivalry. But a narcissist as a sibling is more than just rivalry, it's torture. Sibling rivalry is about competition for resources, whether it's attention, material things, or food. None is more well-known than the biblical story of Joseph from the Book of Genesis, later popularized by Sir Andrew Lloyd Webber and Tim Rice in the Broadway musical, *"Joseph & the Amazing Technicolor Dreamcoat."* Basically, Jacob had twelve sons, but Joseph was his favorite as he reminded him of his favorite wife. Joseph was the brother who'd let Jacob know if any of the other brothers were neglecting their chores or did something wrong. Jacob indulged Joseph and bought him a beautiful multi-colored coat when his brothers wore hand-me-downs. More than just his beautiful coat, the brothers were angered by his role as the tattletale and by Joseph's dreams. Joseph tells his brothers of his dreams of ascendency over them. He dreams of eleven stars (the same amount as his brothers) bowing down to his star. He goes on to tell his brothers about his dreams of superiority.

Joseph may have been prophetic, but his delivery lacked sensitivity. Joseph spoke as a typical narcissist. The brothers were jealous and plotted against him. One day, they successfully sold Joseph into slavery in Egypt. The brothers brought Joseph's torn coat to Jacob as proof of his demise. Some people will go to extraordinary lengths to rid themselves of the narcissist in their life.

Siblings present with all the typical characteristics of a narcissist as we've learned.

I spoke with people about their experiences with their narcissist siblings and there were common behaviors that showed up again and again:

COMMON BEHAVIORS

- *Controlling*
- *Self-centered*
- *Likes to play the victim*
- *Jealous*
- *Competitive*
- *Likes to keep score*
- *Argumentative*
- *Manipulative*
- *Liar*
- *Disrespectful*
- *Belittles, demeans, diminishes*

As siblings age, the non-narcissist sibling naturally grows away from the narcissist sibling. More frequently, they will choose to live geographically distant from this person. There is no great bond between siblings as uncomfortable conversations never occur. Real conversations rarely occur. Communication is almost always about the narcissist. They don't ask a lot of questions. They're simply uninterested in anyone else's life. These types of individuals perpetually stay in the shallow end of the pool when it comes to their relationships.

I spoke with Kim about her relationship with one of her brothers. She said she doesn't feel she knows him well. This seems to be a common thread as no one makes a move to connect. The narcissist sibling doesn't want to build a relationship with the non-narcissist sibling, as they view them as unimportant. The non-narcissist sibling doesn't choose to spend time with the narcissist sibling as they find them infuriating, competitive and controlling.

Ironically, Kim's brother doesn't live far away, yet they rarely see each other. She described her brother as a perennial martyr, always busy doing things for others. When they speak, which is rare, he monopolizes the conversation making it all about him. He never asks about her life, her job, or her husband and children. He lets her know in no uncertain terms; his job is of critical importance. He's defined by his career. This behavior makes it unappealing for Kim to continue contact or seek out her brother.

Judy remembers worshipping her brother when they grew up together. She didn't see him as a narcissist. She saw him as her strong, smart big brother. Now, she reflects on his entitlement. She sees the power her parents gave him as the only male child. She now understands he was jealous when she was born. Growing up she thought he liked playing jokes on her. Now she sees those "jokes" as expressions of rage and disrespect.

Cindy comes from a family of six children. All have remained close except one brother whom Cindy considers a narcissist. She told me he's the type of person who can't see a situation from another's perspective. He's caused a lot of problems in the family. He happens to be very successful in his career.

I asked Cindy, what were family get-togethers and holidays like growing up? She told me he was always onstage, literally. The rest of the family laughed about it. They would say, are you done with your presentation? For these individuals, it's an "I'm talking at you not with you," form of communication. Cindy revealed how he's hard to get deep with because he resides in the shallow end. She said you never get the emotional side of him. Of course, he never asks about Cindy's job, family, or life.

Erika had little contact with her sister as an adult. She had no desire to have a relationship with her but never thought of her sister as a narcissist. She knew there was something wrong as her sister always had to be the center of attention. Her sister was the source of most of the family tension. Erika's sister had few friends and never exhibited empathy. When Erika had breast cancer, her sister called after many years of not speaking. Her sister asked Erika how she was. Erika told her she was good as she had a great prognosis. If you must get cancer, this was the best kind to get.

Her sister then immediately launched into how she's in remission for Crohn's disease. As Chapter 2 discusses, narcissists don't exhibit empathy. Everything is a competition, even your health. This was shocking to Erika as she hadn't spoken to her sister in 15 years. She thought she was calling to talk about her cancer, not her sister's issues with Crohn's disease. It's as if they feel obligated to call so it looks appropriate to other people. However, once on the call, they can't express empathy for anyone else and the conversation must shift to them. Narcissists need to accomplish the task of calling as they feel it will make them look better. It never feels genuine because they can't express real feelings.

I asked Erika if she remembered a particular family holiday or get-together with her sister. Erika reflected on the time when she finally decided she had enough of her sister's behavior. All the sisters gathered at their parent's home with their respective families. Erika lived the farthest away and drove over eight hours with her young family. Erika's narcissist sister always made an entrance. She was suddenly allergic to whatever their mother was cooking or on a new "special diet." She knew how to push everyone's buttons and took every opportunity to push them with abandon.

This holiday, Erika's mother wanted to give her some special teacups. Her sister couldn't stand it, why were they for Erika? The sister started yelling, crying, and carrying on in a narcissistic rage storm. Erika went into another room to cry as she didn't want her young children to see her in tears. This was the moment Erika decided she'd had enough. She decided to no longer attend family gatherings if this sister was included. Unfortunately, Erika's parents never intervened when the sister exhibited these behaviors. This made Erika feel they chose her narcissist sister over her.

Jake always thought his brother was difficult and unpleasant to be around, but not narcissistic. His brother had a weird competitive streak. He would ask Jake about work or what he was doing. But before Jake could even answer, the brother would interrupt and share something above and beyond what Jake said. Once, Jake mentioned he was going hunting soon and his brother chimed in about his plans for expensive, exotic hunting trips to Colorado and Montana to diminish Jake's plans. It felt like he was always in competition with his brother, even when Jake didn't engage.

Jake said sometimes his brother would brag about improbable things like a perpetual one-upmanship contest. His brother would randomly ask Jake what kind of car he drove only to tell him he was about to buy a Mercedes even though it wasn't in his budget. As we know, narcissists have grandiose fantasies and perceive themselves as special and important. Jake's brother needed to remind him of these facts regularly. Once, while Jake was in law school, he visited his family. He was sharing stories about people he met at school with his brother. One was a former Navy Seal.

Well, Jake's brother interrupted that he knew a guy who was not just a Seal, he lived up the street and drove a Ferrari and his wife drove a Land Rover. He kept going on and on. All Jake was doing was sharing stories about people he met in law school. Jake now realizes his brother has lots of "friends," one more fabulous than the next.

With the advent of aging parents and all the issues it brings, Jake's brother has positioned himself as the family savior. He's not the oldest, the most educated nor does he hold the highest professional position. Yet, he has all the answers and seems to believe he's the best person to solve every problem, regardless of his lack of experience or expertise. This assumption of brilliance or wisdom brings all the attention back to him. He needs to be in control and doesn't like challenges, typical of a narcissist. If challenged, he easily employs the narcissist tactics of gaslighting, the silent treatment, or triangulation. Jake's frustration with his brother has led to a strained, distant relationship. They speak a couple of times a year and only see each other at funerals and weddings. It's sad but necessary for Jake.

According to Psychology Today, when dealing with toxic family members, "Sometimes the safer, easier route is to avoid confrontation." However, if you must engage, the article recommends taking a few conscious steps to protect yourself. It's important to ask yourself what are you trying to achieve? If you have a clear vision of your goals and your plan, then you may become less entangled in the minutia of their toxicity. Protect yourself and engage as little as possible with the narcissistic sibling. You can't win with a narcissist. The coping mechanisms are like those with a toxic boss. You should stay focused on the task at hand. Avoiding confrontation isn't a sign of weakness, it shows you are in control of your emotions and your stress levels. You need to take comfort as this is only a temporary situation. You no longer live with these people, and you will not be directly involved with them on a daily basis forever, even though it feels that way. Think about ways to maintain your boundaries. Usually, the best way to protect your boundaries is by going no-contact. This isn't easy when you are dealing with these people in a specific situation. You will need to proactively set time limits, giving these people specific blocks when you are available. It's recommended to compromise with your siblings to mitigate drama, but you absolutely cannot accept any kind of physical or emotional abuse from them. This is non-negotiable. Sometimes it's easier to think of your narcissistic siblings as difficult people at work whom you must work with. Remember, you're in control of your emotions, you no longer live with them, and this situation won't last forever. You'll be able to go back to a no-contact relationship with them soon. These steps will help you manage this difficult time while maintaining control and protection of yourself.

Dr. Ramani Durvasula, a clinical psychologist, says this is one of the most difficult relationships to lose as, "your sibling is your only shared historian." This makes it more painful to cut contact as is the prescribed method of successfully dealing with a narcissist. You'll need to grieve the loss of this relationship. The people I spoke with see their narcissist siblings very rarely, mostly at weddings or funerals. They don't choose to gather on purpose, especially after the parents pass away. Even though they're siblings, they lead separate lives which rarely intersect.

Celebrities are often called out as narcissists at various times in their careers. It's a generality to say all celebrities are narcissists. However, certain individuals demonstrate the characteristics as defined in Chapter 2.

Pop icon Madonna is one of those people. I'm not diagnosing Madonna as a narcissist, but she's exhibited the following:

MADONNA

- *Doesn't like being around other celebrities as she must be the center of attention*
- *Will do anything to attract attention – exhibitionist, envelope-pusher*
- *Surrounds herself with "yes" people to feed her ego and be her supply*
- *Likes to hold grudges*
- *She made a tribute to Michael Jackson on the MTV Awards all about her (she began her speech honoring Jackson at the 2009 MTV Video Music Awards by comparing him to herself: "Okay, here we go again. Michael Jackson was born in August 1958. So was I. Michael Jackson grew up in the suburbs of the Midwest. So did I. Michael Jackson had eight brothers and sisters. So do I.")*

So, what happened with Madonna and her younger brother Christopher Ciccone? It seems early in her career she hired Christopher to be an assistant, concert tour director, and art director. Perhaps as her career skyrocketed, she wanted someone she knew and could trust close to her. However, in this type of relationship where one sibling is so successful and the other is subordinate, it's easy to see where there can be problems. We'll never know what transpired but Christopher wrote a tell-all book after things deteriorated between them. After more than fifteen years working for her, she accused him of theft, her new beau Guy Richie didn't like him, and she didn't select him as her new tour director.

Maybe Christopher wanted recognition of his own, to break out of his famous sister's shadow. Maybe he sought revenge after years of abuse. He performed the lowest of tasks for her, dressing her, being there for her, being her person 24/7 because he loved her, idolized her, and wanted the best for her. But he also wanted to maintain his dignity.

She was unconcerned with his needs; her needs had to be met. If he wouldn't help her, someone else would. After years of feeling taken advantage of, demeaned, disrespected, and uncompensated, he sought catharsis in a tell-all book, looking for recognition for his hard work. When the book was released, it was too late. Narcissists never want negative attention. The Ciccone siblings now live their lives apart.

Perhaps siblings fall out of love with each other when there's an imbalance of power, success, or simply when one is a narcissist.

The relationship between siblings Michael and Fredo Corleone is famously explored in the movie "Godfather Part II." In this reference, I'd argue the narcissist is Fredo, not Michael Corleone. He presents as a covert narcissist. While Michael assumes the godfather role after his father's passing,

Fredo is older and feels he should've been considered. Fredo spends a great deal of time pondering what should've been his. He has such anger and resentment towards Michael, jealousy oozes from every pore.

Fredo is a chronic malcontent who lacks the charisma of his brothers like the characteristics listed in Chapter 7 about Covert Narcissists. He's green with envy over the power his brother Michael wields. He never considers what's best for the family, he only thinks about elevating himself. Fredo tries to assert himself in the family but makes several wrong choices. After Michael becomes the godfather, he confronts the person who's bullied Fredo and strikes him, standing up for his brother. Fredo, with his misguided loyalty and passive-aggressive behavior, gets vocally angry with Michael as a result. Michael, in turn, castigates Fredo for openly taking sides against the family, warning him to never do so again. Fredo takes this public shellacking badly and their relationship goes down a road of mistrust. Fredo tries to manipulate Michael, failing every time. When he finally consorts with a rival family to plot Michael's death, Michael discovers it. Michael realizes Fredo is the family traitor and there's no possible recovery. This is a Hollywood example of a poor sibling relationship taken to the extreme. Michael finally has Fredo killed.

In the movie "America's Sweethearts," A-list actresses Julia Roberts and Catherine Zeta-Jones star as sisters, Kiki & Gwen. Gwen is a big movie star and Kiki is her personal assistant. Gwen is portrayed as a narcissist.

GWEN: *"Nobody knows what it is like being me. Did we brush my teeth?"*

The hijinks ensue when Gwen's former love shows up to promote their last movie together and Kiki falls in love with Gwen's former love. Kiki has reached her limit working for Gwen:

KIKI: (*imitating Gwen*) *"Kiki? Kiki-kins? Is that smoke? Is someone smoking within a six-mile radius of me? Have them put it out! Kiki, my butter has touched another food! I need new butter!"*

This fictitious, humorous example sounds much like what may have occurred with Madonna and her brother, Chris. It's probably not a great idea to work for your sibling if they're a narcissist.

WHAT HAVE YOU LEARNED?

If you have a narcissistic sibling, you've probably known for quite a while. They've been competing with you even when you didn't engage or trigger them. They can do anything better than you can. They've been bragging about their grandiose lifestyle, whether real or imagined. They always have the right answer. They're always triangulating your family, pitting two against one to win their argument or prove their point. They aren't interested in your life, career, or family. It must be lonely and exhausting to be them.

It's sad to realize the instant best friend who was there most of your life, shared family vacations, holidays, hard times, good times, is just not that close anymore. Everyone wants a good relationship with family members, but when they leave you feeling awful about every interaction and dreading the next one, you wonder if you have toxic, narcissistic siblings. At some point, for your own sake, no-contact is the best solution.

GASLIGHTING: MORE LIKE POURING GAS ON THE FIRE

"How many narcissists does it take to screw in a lightbulb? None, they don't use lightbulbs, they use gaslighting."

Anonymous

WHAT IS GASLIGHTING?

Narcissists cleverly manipulate our understanding and interpretation of events to a point where their "victims" literally don't trust their own judgment. As a technique, it's meant to disorient and make people question their very perception of reality. Gaslighting is a powerful sign and a huge red flag that you're in the middle of a toxic relationship with a narcissist.

Gaslighting is defined as, "an elaborate and insidious technique of deception and psychological manipulation, usually practiced by a single deceiver, or 'gaslighter,' on a single victim over an extended period. Its effect is to gradually undermine the victim's confidence in his own ability to distinguish truth from falsehood, right from wrong, or reality from appearance, thereby rendering him pathologically dependent on the gaslighter in his thinking or feelings."

In her book, *The Gaslight Effect*, Dr. Robin Stern defines gaslighting as, "a type of emotional manipulation in which a gaslighter tries to convince you that you're misremembering, misunderstanding, or misinterpreting your own behavior or motivations, thus creating doubt in your mind that leaves you vulnerable and confused." The term originates from the 1944 film titled "Gaslight" where the main character's husband slowly manipulates her to make her believe she's going mad. The film's title originates from the gas lights used in the apartment in the film. The husband uses the gas lights in an upstairs apartment which causes the lights in his apartment to dim. The wife asks her husband about the dimming lights. He convinces her it's merely her imagination, making her feel insane which is a primary intention of gaslighting.

At its core, gaslighting is a formidable tool of manipulation so narcissists can inflict emotional abuse on their victims.

11 WARNING SIGNS OF PEOPLE WHO GASLIGHT, ACCORDING TO PSYCHOLOGY TODAY.

1. Tell blatant lies

2. Deny they said something even if you have proof.

3. Use what you love as ammunition against you.

4. Wear you down over time as you question your own judgment

5. Actions don't match their words. (I love controlling you.)

6. Throw in positive reinforcement to confuse you.

7. Know repeated confusion weakens people's perceptions.

8. Project their weaknesses or failings on others

9. Try to turn people in your circle against you.

10. Tell you or others that you're crazy.

11. Tell you everyone else is a liar.

All types of narcissists employ the tactic of gaslighting to control: employers, parents, friends, spouses, and partners. This strategy's success often depends on the balance of power between two people in a relationship. The tactic reinforces the narcissist's need to be right, be in control and be superior to his victim. Many popular movies have showcased this type of emotional abuse without ever labeling it as gaslighting. Once you're aware of the characteristics, you'll easily see the signs everywhere. Some of the most popular examples of gaslighting include the Disney® animated feature film, "Tangled," thriller adaptation from book to screen of, "Girl on the Train" and shockingly, my beloved romantic comedy, "Overboard."

THESE FILMS SHARE THREE FUNDAMENTAL GASLIGHTING BENCHMARKS:

1. Victims gradually come to doubt their own sanity and feel they can't rely on their own good judgment.

2. Undermining the victim's beliefs and instincts – which makes them think they're weak and fragile.

3. Manipulation of their victims is achieved with their words and the delivery of these words.

"Tangled," an animated Disney® movie, retells the classic fairytale of Rapunzel created by the Brothers Grimm. The Grimm tale is about a couple in love and desperate for a child. Finally, pregnant, the wife only craves lettuce which grows in the yard of their mean, evil neighbor. The husband steals the lettuce (known as rapunzel in German). The neighbor catches the husband and curses him that she will take the child after it's born and leave. The child is a girl, and the evil neighbor whisks her away. She is kept in a tower.

In the Disney® retelling, the dynamic between Rapunzel and her captor, known as Mother Gothel is embellished, reflecting her assumed role as a true narcissist parent who continuously gaslights her kidnapped daughter, Rapunzel. Rapunzel is a princess, stolen from her royal family. She has occasional glimpses of memories from her past life, but they're quickly shut down by her controlling captor/mother.

Mother Gothel tells Rapunzel how she knows best in the song, "Mother Knows Best," filled with examples of gaslighting. In the song, she artfully praises Rapunzel while belittling her at the same time. She tells Rapunzel about all the hidden evils "in the scary world out there." She ties it all together by telling Rapunzel she won't survive out there with a chorus of "Mother knows best." She must keep Rapunzel in the tower to use her magical hair for Mother Gothel's own anti-aging needs. To keep her entrapped, she doesn't employ any physical abuse, she simply uses her words to keep Rapunzel in line. It's a masterful manipulation. She consistently lies to Rapunzel, disparaging her, convincing her daughter she can't survive without Mother Gothel.

SHE ALSO EMPLOYS OTHER TYPICAL NARCISSIST TECHNIQUES INCLUDING:

- *Isolation – in Chapter 10 about romantic relationships you'll see more use of this tactic. Narcissists attempt to isolate you from your circle of friends and family so they can have you all to themselves. This also helps them convince you of their narrative without the distracting truth or interruptions.*

- *Passive-Aggressive wordplay – also called "negging," a term coined by pick-up artists which means negative feedback through back-handed compliments, designed to undermine their victim's self-esteem and self-confidence.*

  Gothel: "How you manage to do that every single day without fail! It looks absolutely exhausting, darling."
  Rapunzel: "Oh, it's nothing."
  Gothel: "Then I don't know why it takes so long!"

- *Victimization – turning the tables. Rapunzel finally musters up enough courage to ask for what she wants, to see the floating lights on her birthday. However, Mother Gothel vehemently denies her request. Then, Mother Gothel goes even further, turning the tables on Rapunzel, making herself the victim, and guilting Rapunzel for being ungrateful.*

At least this movie has a happy ending, and the music is fabulous. Rapunzel manages to live happily ever after. I won't spoil any of the other details for you.

"Girl on the Train" was a best-selling book before it was a feature film released in 2016 starring Emily Blunt and Justin Theroux. The protagonist, Rachel, commutes by train from the suburbs into New York daily, observing people on her way.

Her ex-husband, Tom, is a complete narcissist who can't take responsibility for his actions and who needs to control the narrative, even after Rachel discovers his secret. The movie is a psychological thriller mixed with the complexities of alcoholism. The sad divorcee, Rachel, has witnessed a murder but cannot recall the details as her memories are buried deep in her alcoholic fog. Her ex-husband is quick to question and scoff at any glimpses of her memory, leaving her clinging to the edge of sanity. He exploits her vulnerability and convinces her not to trust her own judgment.

Without spoiling the story, the viewer/reader is made to believe Rachel's drinking and depression made Tom's life hard while he was gaslighting her and supplanting non-existent memories in her mind. Tom mentally and emotionally abuses Rachel, making her believe she is somehow responsible for the horrors in his life.

I've always loved the 1987 movie "Overboard" starring Goldie Hawn and Kurt Russell. I perceived it as a beautiful romance. Now as I've learned much more about narcissism, I see it differently. The main character, Dean, played by Russell, walks out after an acrimonious exchange about his dissatisfactory work which goes unpaid by the other main character, Joanna, played by Hawn when she throws his tools into the ocean. Then Joanna is in an unfortunate accident aboard her magnificent yacht when she goes overboard. She is rescued by fishermen. Dean sees her dilemma reported on the news along with a reward and a plea for information, as she is left with amnesia.

Dean plots revenge and goes to the hospital to claim her as his wife and the reward. This is when the hijinks ensue. He successfully gaslights this woman into thinking she's married to him. Then, he appoints Joanna to raise his four, horribly mannered, feral sons (and his two dogs).

Joanna yields her instincts, becoming a wife to Dean and mother to his children as he basically enslaves her. Dean utilizes all the tools of a gaslighter. When showing Joanna (Annie) her clothes which are not her size, he says her weight has fluctuated over the years with pregnancies and life changes, even though the clothes are also too long for her. When Joanna asks why she looks annoyed in her doctored-up wedding photos, Dean quickly replies, *"Oh, well your dad showed up shit-faced. He threw potato salad all over my mom. It was horrible, we had to throw him out."*

He puts her through the wringer dumping household chores, motherly duties, and more on Joanna. He abuses his power and perpetually exhibits gaslighting behavior. Then they gradually fall in love and live happily ever after, as one does in the movies. When Joanna's real husband finally appears to claim her, the jig is up.

The online magazine, *Birth. Movies. Death.* has called the film, "the most heartwarming rom-com about gaslighting ever made."

For most, gaslighting wasn't a commonly discussed psychological term. It certainly wasn't covered in mainstream news, until 2016. Donald J. Trump was running for President of the United States and holding rallies around the country to garner support. At one of these rallies, campaign manager, Corey Lewandowski, assaulted a reporter, in front of witnesses and captured on a phone video. The reporter was grabbed and pulled to the ground as she tried to question Trump following his speech in Florida leaving her bruised and shaken.

What happened next? Instead of acknowledging the event, the Trump campaign doubled down by attacking the victim. Trump tweeted and was quoted as saying "How do you know those bruises weren't there before?" he said. "I'm not a lawyer." Trump continued talking about it on his plane to reporters, "she said she had a bruise on her arm. To me, if you're going to get squeezed, wouldn't you think that she would've yelled out a scream or something if she has bruises on her arm? Take a look at her facial expression. Her facial expression doesn't even change."

Observers noted this was a typical abuser timeline: assault occurs, denial, gaslighting, blame victim all while still claiming innocence. Lewandowski was later charged with battery. Trump continued mocking the reporter at subsequent campaign events and stood by his campaign manager, unwilling to fire him for the assault. Trump subscribes to the typical narcissist script of believing his own lies and committing to them, no matter the consequences. Like all narcissists, he doesn't like being challenged or questioned.

WHAT DOES A TYPICAL GASLIGHTING CONVERSATION/DIALOGUE SOUND LIKE?

Here is a likely conversation between an Innocent (I) and a Narcissist (N) after an argument about the events of the night before.

I: "Last night, you hurt me when you said I looked terrible and then flirted with Petunia all evening."

N: "I never said that. You have a terrible memory."

I: "You told me when we got to the bar, I looked terrible, like I hadn't spent any time on getting ready."

N: "You're just being paranoid. That never happened."

I: "What about your flirting with Petunia all night?"

N: "Stop being so dramatic. I wasn't flirting with her. You're exaggerating."

I: "Then why did Bob say something to me about it?"

N: "Bob's just jealous of me. I was just joking. Can't you take a joke?"

I: "I don't think it's funny at all."

N: "I'm sorry you think I hurt you. Let's just move on. It's all water under the bridge."

I: "OK. I accept your apology."

N: "Good, if you're lucky, I'll forgive you."

Notice the Narcissist offered a "non-apology apology" where they really don't take responsibility for their actions. They say, *"I'm sorry you think I hurt you,"* when they should say *"I'm sorry I hurt you."* This will sound very familiar if you've ever been in an argument with a narcissist.

When I confronted my father after an argument, I didn't recognize he was gaslighting me, at the time. I repeated back what he said and did. First, he responded, it was a misinterpretation. He wouldn't explain what was misinterpreted or who misinterpreted what. Then he said it was a joke. This should've been a red flag. There was nothing funny about the subject matter or his actions. He never elaborated. He then concocted an elaborate retelling of the facts, including events that never took place. I corroborated his story with the other person involved a true innocent. The innocent, who had no skin in this game, told me none of the above three versions of my father's responses occurred. My father changed the past to fit his recollection – he saw himself as the victim. He was always turning the tables. When he recounts that story, he only remembers it his way, believing all his own lies.

HOW DO YOU RESPOND WHEN YOU RECOGNIZE YOU'RE BEING GASLIT?

Most importantly, in every relationship, trust your own judgment and get an outside perspective. The opinions of other people will validate your concerns and give them gravitas. What you do next depends on who's gaslighting you.

> ***If it's a boyfriend, girlfriend, spouse, friend***: At some point, you must evaluate whether or not you want to stay in the relationship. If you choose to stay, you'll need some evidence because the narcissist will never believe your claims. Take screenshots of texts and emails and use your phone to record conversations. This evidence isn't for legal purposes. It's really for you, to help you realize the person on the other side is a narcissist so you can gain peace of mind. You're not going crazy. You must speak up at some point if you want to remain in the relationship. You also must remain confident and committed to your version of events.
>
> Showing evidence or proof at this point may help convince them to back down. If they decide to argue further, refuse, and stay calm. Refusing to engage in another argument is a way of controlling the situation and protecting yourself. It's important to practice self-care and relaxation techniques. Make sure you have an outlet for yourself both as meditation and

a support network comprised of friends and family. Don't let the narcissist isolate you from them.

Your network will provide emotional support, guidance, a different perspective, and most of all it will give you those precious inner resources essential to your mental and emotional health. If you're suffering emotional abuse, consult a professional. Gaslighting and other techniques of emotional abuse are isolating. Asking for help isn't a weakness. Remember, this isn't your fault. Therapy is constructive, productive, and your business. Take care of yourself first.

If it's a boss or co-worker: If you encounter gaslighting at work, do you just ignore it? Probably not as the narcissist isn't going anywhere and will use this technique to get what he or she wants. Gaslighting is much like bullying. If you react and the narcissist gets what they want, they'll continue. If you can show them their actions don't impact you, the narcissist may move on to another victim. It's important to get evidence with this type of emotional abuse. Record the conversation on your phone and keep copies of emails or text messages. It's equally important to report this behavior to Human Resources and present your evidence to them. You'll need to be strong and call out the abhorrent behavior, while doing it calmly, politely, and professionally. You refuse to tolerate the jokes and backhanded compliments any longer. Remember, gaslighting works because it's confusing and it shakes your confidence. Stand up for yourself and document everything.

If it's a parent: it's not so easy to leave a relationship with a parent compared to the above-referenced relationships. There's no one to report their behavior to and it can make you feel more lost and confused than ever. It's still important to collect evidence of their behavior even to simply give yourself peace of mind. Involving others is also helpful to ground yourself and know that what's happening isn't your fault. I was lucky to have my husband, Joseph who listened to me, validated my feelings, and helped me maintain my sense of sanity.

According to Dr. Robin Stern's book mentioned at the beginning of this chapter, there are five ways to turn off the gas, so this person can no longer gaslight you.

1.   Sort out the truth from the distortion.

2.   Decide whether the conversation is truly a power struggle. If it is, choose to opt out.

3.   Identify both your gaslight triggers and his.

4.   Focus on feelings instead of what you think is "right" and "wrong."

5.   Remember you can't control anyone's opinion—even if you're right.

WHAT HAVE YOU LEARNED?

Gaslighting is a technique of manipulation narcissists use to distort our perception of reality. They use this to control, both the situation and the other person for their own needs. The term "gaslighting" originated from the film of the same name in 1944.

The constant back-and-forth, arguing with a narcissist is exhausting. Once you recognize the symptoms of gaslighting, you'll need to break the cycle and stop the madness. Gaslighting is common with narcissists since their issues are deeply rooted in insecurity and low self-esteem. This particular form of manipulation isolates their victims. Over time, gaslighting can cause you to doubt yourself, second guess your opinions and perceptions and withdraw socially. Gaslighting isn't only used in romantic relationships. This form of manipulation is used by friends, parents, and co-workers or bosses. The technique, however, is the same across all relationships. It's all about control and the balance of power between two people in a relationship. Remember, gaslighting works as a form of emotional and psychological abuse because it's confusing. It makes people question their judgment, their memories, and even their sanity.

When it happened to me, I drew on all my inner resources. I consulted my support network. I needed the support to help me understand this wasn't my fault. I was sure it couldn't possibly be happening. I read and re-read his emails and texts trying to understand why he would double down on the lies. Years after this argument and subsequent gaslighting, he mentioned something about it and managed to maintain his distorted recollection of the events years later. He completely committed to his new reality because it served his purpose.

Gaslighting eliminates the hope of ever having a fair fight. Possessing high emotional intelligence provides us with the strongest tools to resolve conflict, express concerns, and communicate them. Narcissists don't possess these tools. Manipulation is their tool to maintain control and make themselves feel superior. Your best reflex is to be educated and aware of the narcissist, the signs of gaslighting, and refuse to engage. The best defense is to walk away. You'll win your peace of mind and that's priceless.

ROMANTIC HEART-WRENCHING RELATIONSHIPS THAT RAVAGE

RED FLAGS IN ROMANTIC RELATIONSHIPS WITH A NARCISSIST

"My narcissist and I got divorced because of religious differences. He thought he was G-d, and I disagreed."

Anonymous

What happens in a relationship when a man presents himself as Prince Charming and ends up acting more like Tony Soprano? Everyone knows the ideal man – he's the charming and sexy Prince Charming, practically perfect in every way. Like the earlier description of Narcissus, he's physically attractive. Picture him six feet tall, muscular with a shock of thick hair, chiseled jaw, and piercing eyes you could fall into like the ocean. He acts chivalrous and puts his new lady love first, opening doors and slaying dragons for her. He's complimentary, easy to get along with, perhaps even "love bombs" his partner. According to Psychology Today, love bombing is a manner of smothering the object of affection with acts of intense interest and devotion. These can come in the form of love notes, texts, phone calls, gifts, flowers, etc. Narcissists are highly skilled at manipulation and want you to love them. They may even go as far as stalking.

YOU MAY WONDER:

- *What does the beginning of a relationship with a narcissist look like?*
- *When do things typically change?*

The answer to these questions along with insight gleaned from former partners of narcissists will be revealed. I wanted to talk with people who've experienced narcissism in romantic relationships and marriage. I found a small group of women who had very different encounters, yet they were all sickeningly the same. These are real stories. In my interviews with women who fell in love with these men, I discovered a great deal about these relationships. These toxic relationships are not gender-specific by any means. Narcissists come in all forms, in all kinds of relationships. It's not that I didn't want to share other kinds of relationships but the people who volunteered to be interviewed happened to be women in relationships with narcissistic men. Narcissists need to be needed, but on their terms. They need to be superior in the relationship and maintain control. Narcissists truly don't want anyone outside the relationship to know what's happening inside the relationship. They take steps to isolate their partners from family and friends. Often, they do it so slowly and deliberately, the change is almost imperceptible to their partner. They frequently use the technique of gaslighting to make their partner question herself, question events that have transpired and even question her sanity. Slowly, Prince Charming transforms into Tony Soprano, the fictitious television mafia boss who demonstrates the typical signs of narcissism on the show "The Sopranos."

TONY IS:

- *self-centered*
- *emotionally unavailable*
- *lacks the ability to exhibit empathy*
- *doesn't care whom he hurts*
- *abhors criticism*
- *uses people for his own needs*
- *seeks love from multiple women and worse*

Ask Tony, *"who do you think you are?"* He will respond with, *"I'm the person who says how things go, that's who I think I am."* He's a model of what women don't want in a mate. I thought I'd give you fresh reminders going back to Chapter 2 with some red flags. The red flags identify narcissistic characteristics. ►

LOVE AT FIRST SIGHT OR WHEN WE FIRST MET

The dreamy, over-the-top romance is what attracts so many people to fall for the narcissist. Imagining the day when a significant other would rescue them from their dull home life, Linda waited for him. When he appeared, good-looking, several years older, with a car, she jumped into a relationship with him and never looked back. Linda wanted someone to save her, and he was happy to oblige.

Beth believed her compassion and strong sense of empathy attracted him. He had a story of woe and she bought into it – hook, line, and sinker. She wanted to help him and be his friend. He continued his mission of love bombing, purchasing gifts for Beth, and providing special things well beyond her budget. He made her feel like a princess. She felt his adoration. He even accompanied her to a work event where he obsessively watched her the entire time. Beth found his behavior kind of cute. Never before had a guy paid so much attention to her. Beth bought into the whole package.

Jessica fell madly in love with him when they were teens as they shared similar backgrounds and the same religion. She recalls just wanting to be married and start a family with someone who wanted her.

Rebecca experienced an intense physical attraction with her narcissist. He was disarmingly handsome in his expensive suits as if he stepped out of the pages of a magazine. He had a successful corporate career, an MBA, and wanted to marry Rebecca. What could go wrong?

Lucy didn't come from a place of love. This man was so charming, telling her he loved her all the time, day, and night. Lucy deeply wanted him, as she never had this type of relationship and such a feeling of being loved.

When Judy met him, he exuded both confidence and charisma. He seduced Judy with his looks and made Judy feel special. She didn't see it coming.

Dominique remembers his charisma, his charm, and his loving ways at the beginning. He put her up on a pedestal. Once the narcissist feels you're hooked, everything starts to change. Then you begin to see their true stripes.

WHEN DOES PRINCE CHARMING STOP BEING CHARMING AND WHY?

Having children, being around other people as a couple, sensing your new independence, or not feeding their ego enough can all trigger narcissistic responses. Beth was tipped off by his lack of ▶empathy for her and their children. She always felt she was the personality of the two of them. If he was looking to impress someone, he always made sure she was along to do the talking. Looking back, Beth realized everything was always about him. ▶All attention and praise had to be directed at him.

Lucy took classes to learn what was wrong with him. She realized something wasn't right, but she didn't understand the problem. He seemed to enjoy ▶ demeaning her in front of other people while out to dinner. Once he told her she looked homeless compared to the woman they were dining with.

Dominique recognized it was all a game with him. She gradually came to compare the relationship to a lyric from a Fleetwood Mac song, "players only love you when they're playing." She knew if she played along and ▶idolized him enough, everything would be fine. The whole relationship started to change when Dominique began coming into her own power. No longer would she accept him belittling her accomplishments and she started talking back. She always had a plan to escape. She went back to school, completed her degree, and got a good job. He vacillated between bragging about her achievements and belittling her. ▶One minute he was bragging to other people about her. The next minute he was sarcastically telling her, *"Yeah, you're a big deal."* It was a rollercoaster of emotions for Dominique.

Rebecca found him gorgeous, charming, and polite. Appearances meant everything to him, and Rebecca was his arm candy. She soon discovered bringing him home to family for the holidays meant he'd ceaselessly trumpet his career and accomplishments. ► He couldn't stop gloating over his own magnificence.

These were the triggers for the narcissists. Their stories reveal the behavior narcissists exhibited to woo their mates. However, what happened when they eventually revealed their natural behaviors? How did the women in the examples above respond when their partner finally exhibited his narcissistic behaviors? How did it make them feel?

Linda realized even in the beginning; the relationship was a toxic one. She believed she could fix his bad habits, she thought she could fix him. After a while, she knew he was not her "forever mate" and the marriage was a temporary one. When he demonstrated narcissistic behaviors, she felt she could do nothing right. No matter what she tried, she couldn't fix him or anything. This feeling bled into other aspects of her life and made her feel she couldn't do anything right anywhere. It beat her down. Linda became much quieter when his episodes occurred. She said nothing because she knew any response would cause him to react even more. During an argument, he kept score of all the ways Linda hurt him. He always brought up moments from the past as examples. Linda found she could no longer share experiences with him. Once she told him about an argument at work. He wanted to handle it for her to show her how much he loved her and that he was her protector. She learned not to share any of these experiences. Once he learned about it, her battles became his battles. Essentially, he took away her ability to be upset or angry with others.

Beth's road with her narcissist was a difficult one. She suffered from both severe emotional and physical abuse at the hands of her husband. As a result, she developed severe anxiety, severe depression, and complex post-traumatic stress disorder. The only way for Beth to cope was to take prescription drugs. The medication numbed Beth making it difficult to function as a human being. Over the years, she wanted nothing to do with him. She didn't even want to hear him breathe.

Occasionally, people told Jessica she was too good for him. She focused on their three children, their home, and her career. She didn't think much about his frequent out-of-town trips or dinners out with the guys. Finally, a friend told her it would be a good idea to speak with an attorney, so she did. The attorney asked her questions about his whereabouts she couldn't answer. Jessica became her own private investigator. She discovered money flowing out of their joint checking account, where her paycheck was deposited, into an unknown account. Next, she found a toiletries kit he always took on his trips, pushed way back in the linen closet. It contained only mouthwash and condoms. Everything mushroomed from that point forward. Jessica realized he was a serial cheater and a narcissist. After a Black Friday shopping spree, where she bought holiday gifts for their children all at super-sale prices, he told her she had to return everything because they couldn't afford it. Then he'd go for drinks and a concert. Everything was on his terms and for his benefit.

Dominique knew his reputation as a womanizer before they married and thought she could change him. He was highly successful, financially independent, and politically connected. He was the epitome of a very important person. Dominique had all the trappings of a nice life. Things started to unravel when she returned to school and got her degree and a good job. This gave her the confidence to talk back when he belittled her. ►

Instead, he accused her of being selfish and self-centered! He cried, *"I live my whole life around you."* But Dominique knew she did everything for him. She cooked every dish he asked for, hosted everyone he invited to their home, but *she* was the selfish one? Sometimes, Dominique thought, maybe I am the selfish one. She suggested they go to counseling, and he refused. He didn't want anyone else knowing what was happening in their marriage. He wanted complete control.

Lucy grew up feeling unloved and was taught her role was to be a servant for a man. When she met him, she fell madly in love. He was charming, kind, and she fell for it. She realized he was a narcissist in little ways that kept repeating. He always had to be the important person in every situation. He spoke for her in public, even if he didn't know the answer. He ordered food for her in restaurants, never let her drive, and never introduced her to people at events.

Gradually his suffocating actions made Lucy feel she might have a stroke or a heart attack. Daily she felt like a truck was running over her. Lucy saw evidence of his cheating on his text messages. He denied her accusations. These were explicit texts she couldn't forget. At first, he didn't respond at all, completely ignoring her in silence. Then he began aggressively bullying Lucy. At the end of the day, his retort was everything was her fault because she deserved to be cheated on. He turned the table making him the victim, ▶ manipulating the situation.

Judy compared her marriage to her ex-husband to the old story of the frog being boiled alive, unaware of what was happening. Her marriage was emotionally abusive. He bullied her with his crazy antics always focused on maintaining control and ▶ manipulating situations. Judy compared his behavior to general crazy making. She likened him to the character Pigpen from the Peanuts Comics® with a cloud of ever-present dust and dirt swirling around him. He had chaotic energy constantly swirling around him. He always turned things around and spun the story to make him look like the victim. ▶

The first time Rebecca's husband asked for a divorce was on the last day of their idyllic honeymoon on Maui. This became his go-to response when things didn't go his way. He continued asking for a divorce about once a month. The first time, she was stunned, hurt, and in tears. After he said it repeatedly, it became less shocking. Rebecca felt he saw her as not good enough because she made less money than him. He said her journalism degree was stupid. ▶ He had an MBA and was successful in the corporate world. He was completely unsupportive of Rebecca's desire to become a writer. His charming personality appeared again in glimpses throughout their marriage, but Rebecca often witnessed his Dr. Jekyll and Mr. Hyde transformation. He became less charming as they stayed together.

DID THEY DEVELOP COPING MECHANISMS?

Over time, Rebecca developed a thick skin, like elephant hide, as her coping mechanism. This didn't prevent her from sinking into a deep depression over time, making it difficult to get out of bed in the morning. The longer she stayed with him, the less self-esteem Rebecca maintained.

Jessica had no coping mechanisms. When he went into his "narcissistic spin," she felt completely defeated. He pounded the message into her head that everything was her fault. Over time, she felt 100 percent sure he must be right.

Dominique first tried to appease him. She'd try to figure out what was wrong and apologize. Then, there were times she just sat in the bathtub and sobbed. He knew when he got a rise out of her, but he also knew he couldn't get that result all the time. He'd return, and she'd become quiet and sullen. Then he'd show up with jewelry or take her out somewhere special, trying to make it up to her.

WERE THESE WOMEN EVER "GASLIGHTED" BY HIM?

As described in Chapter 9 gaslighting is frequently used by narcissists to change the facts and make the victim feel they're losing their mind.

Jessica now realizes he frequently gaslit her or the kids. After her father passed away, he would say she changed. He said she was difficult to live with since losing her father. He was a gambling addict, a serial cheater, and a narcissist. She never communicated this to their children. They discovered his true nature all on their own.

Once, he explained to their son, he didn't actually have a gambling problem. He lied, telling him Jessica misguided the children about their finances. It wasn't due to his frequent casino visits; it was because Jessica constantly bought clothes and shoes for the kids. The son was confused. His only pair of sneakers were frayed and worn until they had holes. Only then did Jessica buy him another pair. That conversation resulted in him losing the relationship with their son. He told Jessica her spending did so much damage to their finances he was contemplating suicide. Everything was her fault. ➤

Beth experienced gaslighting when they lived in the Northeast. They were expecting a terrible snowstorm and he was a military commander on high alert. Beth walked past the large living room picture window and remarked the storm was here as it started snowing.

He got up from where he was sitting on the couch and walked to the window. Now, both were standing at the window looking out at the white snow pelting down. He looked at Beth and said, *"No, it's not snowing."*

THE 5 STEPS OF NARCISSIST DATING

1. Charm & Seduce
2. Alternate Cruel & Kind
3. Belittle, Abuse & Mock
4. Write off & Reject
5. Rinse & Repeat

OCCASIONALLY, NARCISSISTS PROVIDE A GLIMPSE INTO THEIR REALITY.

Beth once asked her narcissistic husband what was he passionate about? He became completely frustrated with her when her attention was on anything other than him. She had hobbies and interests she enjoyed by herself or with her children. He would get upset as a result. Beth finally asked him, *"what are you passionate about?"* She hoped he might reply; she and the family were his passions. Instead, he sat for a long time with a blank look on his face and said nothing.

One night, he and Lucy went to a dinner event for her real estate association. She was surprised to discover they were honoring her with an important award. She accepted it on stage and thanked everyone, including him. When she returned to the table, he was so jealous, he couldn't even look her in the eye. ►He told her it was time to leave, never congratulating her or taking a picture of her with her award.

Later, he said, *"I don't understand how you were honored in front of the entire community. I've lived here my whole life and never received anything. What's wrong with this picture?"* In a sadistic twist added, *"Maybe I have to be a former refugee like you to be honored."* He couldn't handle the spotlight shining on anyone but him.

WHAT DID YOU LEARN? WHAT TO DO IF YOU FIND YOURSELF IN A RELATIONSHIP WITH A NARCISSIST?

Judy recommends getting out of a relationship with a narcissist as soon as you discover the truth about them. It's much harder to get out after having children together. She finally gathered the strength and power to stand up and leave. For her, it was the biggest, most profound thing she'd done up to that point, refusing to let his drama and games hook her. He wasn't accustomed to anyone standing up to him. There was no reasoning with him because he always believed he was right. She stood up to him by not engaging or playing his games. She even hung up the phone on him once. When she was finally out of the relationship, she felt even more powerful.

Linda realized years after their divorce, his problems had nothing to do with her. When she finally got up the nerve to ask for a divorce, after thinking about it for three years, he blamed her. He told her she destroyed his life. He married twice more after they divorced and was engaged several times too, but he never got over Linda.

The last time Rebecca's husband asked for a divorce after doing it dozens of times, she didn't answer. She just walked upstairs and packed a bag. On her way out the door, he said, *"we can talk things out."* She turned the knob and kept going. After the five years they spent together, through the heartache and the love, she still believes he gave the best he could. She saw him as a deeply wounded person, the walking wounded.

Sadly, this is a basic truth of all narcissists – hurt people hurt other people. All the narcissists profiled in this chapter came from places of hurt. They were either abandoned or emotionally or physically abused themselves. They were stuck in an emotional glitch with no escape. They never recognized or acknowledged the damage they did to others. They just keep glitching.

These were all bright, intelligent women who tolerated a great deal because they loved these men and thought they could change and become better husbands and fathers. In every one of their stories, there were redeeming values to each "him." Each woman fell in love. Sometimes, it was a case of co-dependency where they needed to be needed. Sometimes, they sought a rescuer. Every time, it ended badly.

None of them deserved the result they got. All of them see their life as far better now with their narcissist in the rearview mirror. Dominique said when you're in a relationship with a narcissist, it's always bad.

EMOTIONAL GRENADES

WHAT IS AN EMOTIONAL GRENADE?

Emotional grenades are comments or actions typically executed by a narcissist to make a powerful point. Their grenade is lobbed into a discussion or room. The grenade "explodes" causing utter chaos for everyone within earshot. Real military grenades are small missiles containing an explosive or chemical agent projected as a deadly weapon. Emotional grenades don't do physical damage but still create chaos. Narcissists enjoy throwing emotional grenades. Then they flee the scene. My father's an expert at projecting emotional grenades. Sometimes they're tiny, barely noticeable pops and sparks. Other times, the aftershocks feel massive, like being trapped in a war zone spinning out of control.

Many times, I've found myself on the receiving end of projected emotional grenades. However, I still haven't found the best way to deal with them. When I receive an emotional grenade, my first instinct is to hurl one right back. Sometimes it makes me so angry; it's so hurtful, I want to reciprocate the negative sentiments. Perhaps there's a better way to respond. Maybe you can be the bigger person, be the adult in the situation and look past the hurt. Try to understand the narcissist's deep insecurity and lack of self-confidence. It's up to you how you respond but be aware, similar to the narcissist in your life, your actions have repercussions as well.

At the hospital's annual golf tournament, a close friend tells me people are whispering about how I've reacted badly to my father dating. If you live in a larger metropolitan area, you may not understand the significance of this. Small towns are great for raising kids but rife with gossip where everyone knows everyone. He's a big fish in an exceedingly small pond. I've grown up with the benefit of him being "known" as well as the awkward, uncomfortable gossip. My father's lobbed another emotional grenade of gossip. I begged him not to go down this road, yet here we are.

Our dynamic shifts because his words put my professional reputation at risk. I send him an email about what I've heard. Growing up I learned not to air dirty laundry in public. My father's a public persona in our small community and my mother fastidiously kept private. Now, I had to prepare to answer random questions about him at work, which made me even more uncomfortable.

It felt like being a reality show contestant: "Mom's Dead, Dad's Dating and Daughter's Dumbfounded – Watch What Happens Next!" The show features enormous levels of humiliation, living out ultra-personal situations for the viewing public's entertainment. Haven't seen a reality show so sadistic since Real Housewives!

He responds with an email neither admitting nor denying responsibility. He uses sweeping generalities as if everything he does is bad, more "splitting." Then he goes on to recite his resume. A true narcissist, he uses the word "I" 47 times.

What does his resume have to do with gossip floating around town? I asked why he'd air our private issues in public. He replied with a list of everything he does. It seems he's decided since everything he does is bad, why not lean into his "badness" even more? His legacy in our small community has been a driving force throughout my adulthood. As a narcissist, he can't take responsibility for his actions. It would be an admission of guilt. He turns the tables to make it seem like I'm crazy, a classic gaslighting strategy. These are among the examples in Chapter 9 on gaslighting.

I spoke with Patricia who has similar experiences with a narcissistic father. After her parents divorced, her dad began dating. The new girlfriend tried to create drama between Patricia's dad and all his children. The girlfriend was trying to make Patricia's dad think she was against him, making trouble between Patricia and her dad.

During one episode, Patricia had to drive her father somewhere as he couldn't drive. She was about 20 miles into the trip when he asked her what's her problem with the girlfriend? Patricia told her father she didn't have a problem with the girlfriend. The girlfriend has a problem with all the kids. She's not nice. He then threw the scotch he was drinking at Patricia as she drove. The scotch went in her ear, in her eye, and down her face. Patricia promptly turned the car around at the next exit and started for home.

Her father started to cry – don't go home and tell your husband. Don't tell him. He was embarrassed at his behavior and didn't want Patricia's husband to know.

With my father, I'm still trying to make our family equation work. You may think why even contemplate it? I don't want to eliminate him from our family. So, when he offered to take our family to the Dominican Republic for Christmas week, all-inclusive, we skeptically agreed. We all enjoyed the one-week trip to a beautiful resort. We liked it so much and things were stable the following year, so we went again, paying our own airfare. He enjoyed having everyone together, so he asked if we could plan for the third year. We agreed. This time he suggested a two-week trip through the New Year. We had no idea what kind of narcissistic temper tantrum was yet to come.

As Chapter 2 illustrates, narcissists feel preoccupied with fantasies of unlimited power, success, intelligence, and achievements. They require excessive admiration and attention. The Mayo Clinic highlights common behaviors typical in narcissists like experiencing trouble handling anything viewed as criticism.

THEY OFTEN:

- *Become impatient or angry when they don't receive special treatment*
- *Have significant interpersonal problems and easily feel slighted*

- *React with rage or contempt, belittling others to appear superior*
- *Have difficulty regulating emotions and behavior*
- *Experience major problems dealing with stress and adapting to change*
- *Feel depressed and moody if they fall short of perfection*
- *Harbor feelings of insecurity, shame, vulnerability, and humiliation*

This was the blueprint for our family vacation from hell. On the menu were varying degrees of emotional grenades, from flares of rage to the silent treatment. This trip wasn't nearly as comical as National Lampoon's Vacation movies, yet it was a perfect storm of dysfunction served with unlimited alcoholic beverages.

The resort was a timeshare-style property we'd already bought into by now. They liked pitching owners on buying more options every year. On our third day, Joseph, my father, and I attended an update.

After the pitch, my father looked at Joseph and me and asked if we should continue investing.

I replied we weren't interested in further investments, and it wasn't necessary for him either.

This was his cue. After telling him what to do– he promptly made a large financial commitment to the resort. It's his money after all.

I candidly told him Joseph and I didn't have more money to add to the investment. Not only were we unable to contribute but it was unnecessary.

I allowed his charges on my credit cards because he didn't have enough credit to charge the entire amount. The charges added up to more than we had readily available. I agreed with the caveat he'd reimburse us at home. Everything happened so quickly. He never said "thank you" for the charges on my cards and for sticking my neck out.

We returned to our villa to continue our vacation. The next day, agitated and angry, he stopped speaking. We were staying in the same accommodations, eating every meal together and he no longer acknowledged his family. The girls were thirteen and nine years old. Every day became Groundhog Day, repeating the events of the previous day, over and over. We were stuck in a tropical paradise with every imaginable luxury and my father gave us the Silent Treatment.

At first, he acted like a petulant child having an epic tantrum. Then his behavior changed. Each day, he began by sitting outside to read. Once he played music on his phone at the loudest setting as the girls slept.

He wouldn't answer a cheery, *"Good morning."* He only came inside when the cook arrived to make breakfast. He'd greet the cook and ask for his eggs as he liked them. The four of us were talking among ourselves. Then we all went to the beach. He avoided eye contact, only speaking in brief statements or exclamations. He didn't purposely stay away or hole up in his bedroom. He went everywhere with us; he just didn't speak. This might sound like I'm a giant spoiled brat. But like most people, we had limited vacation time and wanted it to be the best it could be. You're in paradise with a person intent on ruining everything. Each day got progressively worse. He was infuriating and frustrating. His cold, calculated actions made him seem like a villainous robot. Nothing I did or said changed his behavior.

When you travel with a group of people you typically communicate where you're going or what you're doing. It's common courtesy. The entire trip he'd get up from a table, a chair, or the beach and silently walk away. He never said where he was going.

As Chapter 2 describes the characteristics of narcissism, one is a complete lack of empathy. Did I ever notice his total disinterest in others' pain? Again, my mother mellowed his idiosyncrasies. She expressed emotion, care, sympathy, empathy, and sensitivity for both of them. He was incapable.

For a few days, I mentioned my knee was throbbing with pain. After an early morning walk, I expressed feeling more intense pain. A normal person would make polite conversation asking, *"how did you hurt it?"* or *"where does it hurt?"* My father couldn't care less. Unless it affects him directly, it's off his radar.

Finally, I was exasperated enough to say, *"a normal person would ask how I injured it."* His retort, *"you've been talking about it all week. What do you want me to say?"* A few months later, I was diagnosed with a torn meniscus needing surgery.

Patricia had a similar experience with her father. After working for him at the family-owned company for years, taking his emotional abuse, Patricia began suffering from severe depression and found it difficult to get out of bed in the morning. She told her father about her condition.

He replied, *"we can't deal with special circumstances."* Like a true narcissist, her father couldn't exhibit empathy for anyone, especially his own children.

On our vacation from hell, we were trapped in the same house for two weeks with a recalcitrant father and grandfather. We still don't know what happened. There was no epic rage storm. He simply shut down. Was this about control? Did he commit to something he shouldn't have? Then felt out of control and dictated how the rest of the trip would go?

This is exactly the behavior referenced in Chapter 2 when comparing narcissistic personality disorder to people with high emotional intelligence. Due to his narcissism, my father has low emotional intelligence.

WHEN HE IS FACED WITH SEVERAL PROBLEMS, HE:

- *Is incapable of communicating his feelings*
- *Unable to regulate his emotions*
- *Feels lost, angry, filled with rage and resentment*
- *Is unhappy with everyone, especially us*
- *Exhibits go-to behaviors of shutting down in a crisis*
- *Makes himself the victim, lashing out at others, and*
- *Is ill-equipped to deal with problems, refusing to ask for help.*

On our last day, we were getting ready to leave. He was nowhere to be found. He'd overslept, so I woke him. He never said thank you. He came to breakfast and announced I'd better find his house key. He was in a terrible mood and let everyone know it. Then he put on huge headphones the rest of the day to avoid speaking to anyone. This is a sign of disrespect that says the narcissist refuses to listen.

Once home again, we had no contact. He didn't reach out to me, and I didn't reach out to him. After 18 days of silence, I emailed him as the credit card bill was due soon. We covered his additional timeshare purchase but didn't have the funds to pay.

He seemed surprised and responded that we should meet, "since our communication hasn't been good since we got home."

He sent me an email stating "It has been 18 days since I have been with my family after a nice vacation." He thought it was a pleasant vacation? His email sounded like he was on a different trip as if he lost touch with reality.

Recently, clinical analysis of narcissists and dissociation was published in the *Journal of Addiction & Addictive Disorders*. It explored the concept of dissociation – how narcissists tend to erase memories. It contends since their interactions are through a fictitious construct: the false self, narcissists often dissociate. My father made a conscious effort to stop talking, making everyone miserable. How did we go on two similar vacations with no problems of this magnitude? What made him snap this time? The most confusing event was he reserved this time for our "nice family vacation" for another five years while not speaking. Why would he want to repeat this disaster? It was the last good trip we took together.

In the movie "Mean Girls," the antagonist is the character, Regina George. All Regina's ideas are unquestionably accepted by her group. She's always the designated leader. When Regina tells a joke, everyone laughs. When Regina declared on Wednesdays they wear pink, everyone did. Regina loved to throw emotional grenades and watch the chaos unfold. Her emotional grenades came in the form of negative rumors about other students and teachers. They reveal she only cares about herself, as a typical narcissist. She feels no guilt about being judgmental, two-faced, or telling people what to do.

When Gretchen, a member of her group, introduces the word "fetch" into their vernacular, Regina won't even pretend to like the word. She tells Gretchen, "Stop trying to make fetch happen. It's not going to happen." There's an uncomfortable shift when Cady joins the group and expresses her opinions. The group begins laughing at Cady's jokes and accepting her ideas.

Regina is put off. She loses her balance, her mojo. Regina portrays a typical narcissist. She craves excessive attention and needs people to follow her directions. She wants to be the leader, adored and envied. When the group stops following Regina's directions, she doesn't feel like herself anymore.

My father needed to be the leader. When he felt no one was taking his directions, he lost his mojo. He demonstrated this by throwing emotional grenades on our vacation and giving the silent treatment. Well-known as a form of emotional abuse, the Silent Treatment is discussed more deeply in Chapter 12.

His was an odd example since we were living together for two weeks yet he ceased all communication.

I finally reached out to him because the credit card payments were looming. We didn't have the funds. The charges weren't even ours.

He replies with an email revealing for the first time the cause of his silent treatment: "Maybe after investing, I thought too much about it as a mistake. I also thought that mom wouldn't have agreed with it, but it was too late." Though he bragged about having plenty of money when the resort asked for another commitment, now the "investment will be questionable." He sees the investment as a mistake my mother would never have agreed to.

Every time, we settle things and I feel better, he introduces a new facet, obstacle, or stumbling block. I just want an open, honest discussion about why he'd tank a family vacation, perhaps to prevent it from happening again. Since Joseph and I have limited vacation time and funds, another trip with him sounds like a nightmare.

Patricia shared with me some of her nightmare vacations with her father. She told me about one family vacation in particular. Patricia had five siblings and their father ran a family company founded by his grandfather. After her parents divorced, she got to take two vacations a year: one to visit her mother and the other to go to Florida with her father. Her father invited all her siblings and their families to go to Florida on the company private plane to a property he owned to pick grapevines and do other work. Most of the trip was work but they all got a small amount of free time. Whenever the kids were given the chance to enjoy themselves, their father was known to ruin the mood. One night, after hanging out at the beach all day, everyone came back to the house. Her father announced he was going to take a nap. Since everyone was hungry and their father was sleeping, Patricia and her siblings assumed he would be happy dinner was ready when he awoke. They cooked all the hot dogs and ate.

Their father woke up from his nap at 8:00 PM and says, *"I got a hankering for a raw hot dog."* Only there are no more raw hot dogs as they thoughtfully cooked them all. OH BOY! IT WAS A BAD NIGHT! He lost his mind. Her father was swearing, angry, throwing things, and yelling. He went into a full-blown rage storm! All because there wasn't a raw hot dog to be had. After they returned home from the trip, their father charged all of them for the airfare on the company plane.

I'm so grateful to have my husband Joseph there to talk to and listen. As I stated in Chapter 1, it's critically important to have a support system. Also, Joseph was witnessing this bad behavior and that was validating for me. In Chapter 9, you read how important the perceptions of others and their support is for you if you're being gaslighted. You need a network to provide you with emotional support, guidance, and inner resources.

To regain peace, I agree to meet with my father. I accept my father's "non-apology" apology and we're back to ground zero. My upset and his actions play in a constant loop in my head, over and over. I need peace to stop the cycle. But we won't take another vacation together.

Now seven years after this nightmare vacation, I reflect on things I could've done to change the situation. Looking back, the trip could've gone differently if I sat down and had a "come to Jesus" discussion with my father. But I didn't understand at the time what was happening or why he was so out of control. Knowing what I know now, I would've confronted him to put a stop to the madness. He didn't have the communication skills then and still doesn't express his frustration or feelings. All my father had was his self-doubt. No one was giving him the narcissistic supply he desperately needed to function. My daughters were too young, and my husband wouldn't have confronted him. It was left to me.

WHAT HAVE YOU LEARNED?

I wanted to maintain a relationship with my father, I was willing to waste precious resources on a vacation with him. This trip finally made his diagnosis crystal clear; he was a narcissist. His need for grandiosity and to be a Very Important Person trumped any need for good family relations. Most people would give anything to have time to spend with their family. Not him. He had an incredible opportunity to talk to, play games with, and have fun with his two granddaughters for two weeks without day-to-day distractions like technology, TV, friends, or school. He chose to read four books and be by himself. He chose to stop talking. We asked him to play games. He turned us down. We stopped asking. We had problems in the past, but I've never seen him behave so badly for so long with no explanation. Once home, he reframed it as a nice family vacation. Perhaps dissociation helps explain how and why he viewed our trip that way. Apparently, he didn't see himself behaving badly due to his false sense of reality.

We didn't cater to him or tell him how great he was for making his investment. We didn't tell him how handsome he looked or how smart he was for reserving a certain restaurant. We didn't ask his opinion about world events. Essentially, in his mind, the failed vacation was our fault.

Clearly, we could've performed better and done the above things. But the four of us are real, genuine, and transparent. We mean what we say and say what we mean. We love being in each other's company. This only angered him more. Narcissists constantly need to be the center of attention, be revered, and admired. We just wanted a father and grandfather. I had no idea his lowest point was still to come.

THE SILENT TREATMENT DAMAGES & DESOLATES

"Just remember when you are ignoring her, you are teaching her to live without you."

Unknown

Silence. Unresolved anger. Abandonment. Cruel and unusual punishment. These are the thoughts that spring to mind when we hear the term "the Silent Treatment."

According to an article on the website GoodTherapy.org, the Silent Treatment is a form of emotional abuse typically used by narcissists.

THE GOALS OF GIVING THE SILENT TREATMENT ARE TO:

1. place the abuser in a position of control

2. silence the target's attempts at assertion

3. avoid conflict resolution/personal responsibility/compromise

4. punish the target for a perceived ego slight.

Usually, the desired result is provoking a reaction from the victim to reinforce the needed sense of control for the narcissist.

Historically, the phrase "Silent Treatment" originated from 19th-century prison reform in the United States. As an alternative to physical punishment, prisoners were rarely spoken to and no longer allowed to speak to each other. The system referred to them as a number instead of their name. They were forced to spend long hours in isolation. The goal was to break their will. Many prisoners went mad as a response to this kind of deprivation. During this time, renowned scholar and author Alexis de Tocqueville was invited to tour this experiment. He was quoted as condemning these silent prisons. "This absolute solitude, if nothing it is beyond the strength of man; it destroys the criminal without intermission and without pity; it does not reform; it kills." This program was soon discontinued in the prison system. Thus, the Silent Treatment is considered too cruel for prisoners. However, narcissists still employ it regularly on their victims.

In the 2017 motion picture "Lady Bird," the Silent Treatment is featured as a tactic of emotional abuse inflicted by a mother, played by Laurie Metcalf, on her daughter played by Saoirse Ronan. The movie's mother-daughter relationship is focused on a mother who's an emotionally abusive parent. Many see the mother as difficult and downright cruel at times. The two women have a complicated relationship. She doesn't show traditional affection, praise, or pride for her daughter, known as Lady Bird. She undermines her daughter's happiness with passive-aggressive remarks and actions, akin to the behaviors of a covert narcissist. Those behaviors are detailed in Chapter 7. The family is from Sacramento and of modest means. Lady Bird's mother always assumed her daughter would attend college in-state. When she learns Lady Bird dared to apply to a college in New York, she cuts off all communication between her and her daughter, even though they live together in the same small home. It's as if a curtain closes and the Silent Treatment begins.

Nothing Lady Bird does – cry, apologize, beg, plead, sob – changes the mother's position. This is the highest level of emotional abuse. The abuse continues for months while Lady Bird begs her mother to acknowledge her. Mother refuses to do so. It's hard to imagine. In a final rejection, the mother accompanies the father to take Lady Bird to the airport. But she still won't acknowledge her daughter. Lady Bird bids goodbye to her mother through the car window. By the time the mother realizes her mistake, Lady Bird is already on the plane on her way to New York. The mother is completely incapable of expressing genuine human emotion to her daughter. Battling her own inner demons, she's caught in a war within her mind. The resulting abuse is hard to watch onscreen. I wanted to hug Lady Bird and tell her everything would be all right. It was like watching my own experience, knowing the feelings of abandonment, loss of a parent, and immense hurt. When the relationship is between a parent/child and the parent gives the child the Silent Treatment, the child can't help but feel out of control, helpless and hopeless. This is true cruelty. There's no communication at all which is extremely tragic.

According to an article in The Atlantic, narcissists use the Silent Treatment to punish and control. Kipling Williams, a psychology professor at Purdue University stated, "people use the Silent Treatment because they can get away with it without looking abusive to others and because it's highly effective in making the targeted individual feel bad." A recent study found a correlation between social rejection and the similar brain activity that results from physical abuse. The study Does rejection hurt? found the anterior cingulate cortex area of the brain, lies on the medial surfaces of the brain's frontal lobes, and encompasses subdivisions that play key roles in cognitive, motor, and emotional processing was active in cases of both emotional and physical abuse. This research suggests victims feel actual physical pain from this type of emotional rejection.

The Atlantic article also noted meting out the Silent Treatment can be addictive for the giver. "The father who couldn't force himself to speak to his son again suffered the way many addicts suffer – through repeating an activity despite knowing its harm. Most people who start giving the Silent Treatment never intend for it to go on as long as it does, but it can be very difficult to stop. It's psychological quicksand." This is like comparing the application of the Silent Treatment to drug addiction. Narcissists become addicted to inflicting this form of emotional abuse as a solution to their own pain. Since narcissists can't regulate their emotions, they also can't process criticism, failure, or defeat in a normal way. Their reactions to crisis or controversy are not normal so their go-to reaction is giving the Silent Treatment. This is especially so if they're without their narcissistic supply to comfort them.

My father is an expert at giving people the Silent Treatment. I've been a witness to him giving it to others as well as to myself for my entire life. Most of the time, he would get angry about some perceived slight, or a perceived offense. Then he would dismiss that person by giving them the Silent Treatment. I never knew how to stop the Silent Treatment once it started. When my mother was alive, she always put an end to it. Without her intervening, there was no one to mediate or talk him into ending this behavior. I didn't know how to say I wanted to resolve a certain issue. I kept asking him to explain his actions and he categorically refused. Experts recommend taking advantage of therapy – group/couples/individual if someone in your life uses the Silent Treatment on you tactically and often. Experts also recommend if this abuse happens for long periods, it might be the right time to leave the relationship.

Many individuals are credited with saying "insanity is doing the same thing over and over again but expecting a different result." The list ranges from Albert Einstein to mystery novelist Rita Mae Brown, to a pamphlet from Narcotics Anonymous circa 1981. Even if Einstein didn't say it, it's a highly logical statement.

DO YOU WONDER:

- *Why do we continue doing the same thing over and over expecting the situation to end differently?*

- *How many times can a parent give a child the Silent Treatment and they will continue going back for more?*

- *How do you maintain a normal relationship with a person when you don't know what might set them off or when they may stop speaking to you?*

- *Why do people keep giving the narcissist more chances when they keep hurting us?*

The Atlantic article concludes, "In the end, whether it lasts four hours or four decades, the Silent Treatment says more about the person doing it than it does about the person receiving it."

I'd wake up in the middle of the night thinking I was having a nightmare where my father refused to speak to me. Then I'd realize it was no nightmare, it was reality. I didn't understand why he shut me out. All I did was ask him to explain his actions. But trying to hold a narcissist accountable is one of the worst things you can do because it backs them into a corner. I didn't realize he was a narcissist and that you can't ask one to do this. I only knew he was supposed to be my father, yet he wouldn't act like it.

There were many times throughout my childhood and adolescence when my father stopped talking to me. I can't even remember what happened to cause most of those experiences. It was a common practice for him to stop speaking to me and others. I remember once I was joking around with him and called him a silly name like "schmoopy." He took offense to it and went to his room to sulk.

This is when my mother would intervene, speaking to each of us individually. She would tell me everything was fine and to just come to dinner. He wouldn't be angry anymore. So, we'd both show up to the dinner she prepared. She would lead the conversation making an effort to get each of us to speak or acknowledge something she said. And then it was over. There was no more discussion about what happened or why. Nothing was ever resolved because she smoothed over all our problems. That is until she passed away and there was no one to intervene and smooth over our problems anymore. Without her presence, we didn't know how to speak to each other. We certainly didn't know what to do when a conflict arose.

The first time my father gave me the Silent Treatment after my mother died, I didn't even realize what was happening. I was still writing off his odd behavior as grief. Then, whenever I veered off script and disagreed with him, he would stop talking to me. These times were brief in duration. Sometimes, I didn't even realize he wasn't speaking to me. Our journey to The Big Silent Treatment began during and after our Dominican Republic vacation from hell. After returning, he didn't speak to me for almost two months. At the end of February 2015, I forgave him again without receiving an apology. He seemed to remember it as a nice vacation with his family. As I've already discussed, this was dissociation, the narcissist's ability to rewrite history to fit his preferences. I didn't realize back then, 2015 was the perfect storm for our relationship. It came because of him losing control without knowing how to regain it. It was like the whole Dominican trip was a gateway drug to the Silent Treatment for my father.

A TIMELINE OF THE SILENT TREATMENT FROM MY FATHER:

January 2015: end of Dominican Republic vacation and almost two months of The Silent Treatment. Strike One.

February 2015: at the end of the month we meet, I forgive him without apology.

March 2015: things are quiet and relatively peaceful; I continue interviewing for a new job.

April 2015: I'm offered a new job and I tell my father. Strike Two.

May 2015: I leave my current job where they honor me in two ways.

June 2015: My father becomes angry and phases in and out of periods of not speaking, but I wouldn't call it a total Silent Treatment episode.

July 2015: I tell my father about the ways my previous employer is honoring me. Strike Three.

August 2015: the CEO from my previous employer tells me what happened.

September 2015: I confront my father. As a result, he stops talking to me. This is full-blown Silent Treatment.

October 2015: we exchange emails but have no personal contact.

November 2015: There are fewer emails and still no personal contact between us.

December 2015: No contact. The Silent Treatment is on.

January 2016: Silent Treatment

February 2016: Silent Treatment

March 2016: Silent Treatment – punctuated with a few emails.

April 2016: Silent Treatment

May 2016: We meet once again. I just want to listen to him and have peace.

September 2016: He stomps out of a restaurant. Silent Treatment through September 2019, over three years.

Now you have a fuller picture of how the events played out over this period and can see the brewing storm. I see the strikes against his ego building up. Remember, we still live in the same small town and tend to run into him at various places. He saw my husband, Joseph at his office and didn't say hello. He saw my daughter, his granddaughter, at the golf course and barely waved. The Silent Treatment is a game where you're punished if you don't stay on the narcissist's script. When I ask why he stopped talking to me this time, instead of answering the question he went into victim mode saying, *"If you don't want a relationship with your father that is your choice. If you do not want me around, I understand."*

Any time I confronted him asking for an explanation of his actions, I got the Silent Treatment. Every time he turned my request into extremes of, *"You don't want me in your life,"* instead of explaining his actions.

I naively asked him to please be present in his relationship with me, Joseph, and the girls. I asked him to make conversation and act like he's glad to see us. I told him it appears his public image is more important than his relationship with us.

As per usual, he would deny it saying he's too old to care about his public image.

More lies. This just doesn't square up with the times he tries to stage a forced public appearance.

In August 2015 – shock and awe. I believe his reactions to the situation I'll describe in Chapter 13 were a culmination of events throughout the year beginning with the Dominican vacation. After confronting him, he didn't speak to me for eight months, as mentioned in the previous chapter. This is Strike Three to his ego. Then in May of 2016, I again listen to him explain the how and the why, all while deflecting and distracting with irrelevant facts and events. He turns the tables repeatedly to make himself the victim. He gaslights me again and again with his perception of what happened. I spent the last year in therapy, learning coping skills and how to reposition myself. All this happened with the intention of protecting myself from the hurt caused by his words and actions. I set out to cultivate a peaceful disinterest with my father.

I was doing well maintaining peaceful disinterest, speaking to him every few weeks, and seeing him about once a month.

Then in September 2016, he invited us to dinner at a local restaurant to celebrate our "wedding anniversary," even though we've never celebrated our anniversary together. Upon arrival, he seemed to be busting his buttons, wanting to share something with me. He carried a shopping bag and pulled out a program. He couldn't wait to tell me he attended the hospital gala the night before. This was the same hospital gala I was responsible for during the 16 years I worked for the hospital. It was also the same one which honored me the year before when he refused to attend and told me he'd *"never do anything with that hospital again."* He brought me the program from the event.

I felt the color drain from my face. His blustering the year before had nothing to do with the hospital or him. He didn't attend because he couldn't stand seeing me honored. Now, after his ultimatums, he went back to the event as if I was a blip on the radar. He looked around the table, seeing my children and husband's confused, silent faces. I looked down in disbelief. We were right back to where we were before. My peaceful disinterest disappeared.

My father finally put two plus two together. He got up and yelled to the waitress, *"I'll take my dinner to go."* Then he walked out of the restaurant and our lives, again.

This time he gave me the Silent Treatment for four months. Then he decided he was ready to meet and be a family again. Only this time I couldn't do it. I couldn't pretend everything was okay. I was shocked, hurt, and done with all of it. We didn't speak or meet again for the next three years, until September 2019.

I reached a point where I reviewed the last two years of our relationship. Meeting with him resolved nothing. History kept repeating itself, but like fresh wounds, it did so in different ways. I realized I couldn't control his actions or behaviors. Nothing changed except the passage of time. He still doesn't understand how the Silent Treatment given for so long and so many instances impacts me. He's basically removed himself from my life as a result. I still feel the loss. The primary way I keep my sanity and sense of happiness is to compartmentalize these feelings and focus on all that's good in my life. I'm grateful for all the positive elements in my life: my husband, my daughters, and my career. These things provide stability and pleasure for me, and they combat the loss.

6 WAYS THE SILENT TREATMENT IS ABUSIVE

Narcissists use silence as a manipulation to control their victims and get them to do their bidding. According to psychcentral. com, they use the Silent Treatment in six different ways.

THEY:

1. Ignore their victim: The traditional way to apply the Silent Treatment is to stop all communication with their chosen victim(s). This behavior dismisses, devalues, and discounts their intended target.

2. Evade or stonewall their victim: The difference between this and the traditional Silent Treatment tactic is the narcissist doesn't completely cut off communication. They won't look their victim in the eye or speak in full sentences. Communication is more of a grunt or a nod, barely acknowledging their victim. This is how my father behaved in the Dominican Republic.

3. Subverting: This is manipulation at its best. The narcissist sabotages their victim's work and success, undermining their victim's power without their knowledge.

4. Rejecting: A tactic used mostly in romantic relationships, the narcissist rejects all physical affection. He or she attempts moving away from their victim, refusing all closeness or intimacy.

5. Quarantining: Isolates the intended victim from friends and family who will no doubt feel empathy toward them. The narcissist wants their victim to suffer from their Silent Treatment alone.

6. Shunning: The highest level of isolation, shunning is isolation from an entire community, organization, or religious group. The narcissist tells lies and misinformation against their victim to the community. They discredit and alienate their victim from the entire community.

The Silent Treatment is a way of withdrawing and withholding love from another person. Imagine the damage this does to a family member. It wears people down, filling them with shame and guilt. It's pure torture. Just the threat of it forces us to walk on eggshells around the narcissist. It's normal behavior of a narcissist who regularly gives the Silent Treatment to expect support from their victims when they're ready to connect again. This was particularly true of my father.

STRATEGIES TO COPE WITH A NARCISSIST GIVING THE SILENT TREATMENT

Once you recognize or acknowledge you're suffering from the Silent Treatment by your narcissist, you have several options in how you respond. Unquestionably, one option is to walk away from the relationship. That may be the right answer for you. Nonetheless, there are other strategies you can employ. They include:

1. Listen Reflectively

Try not to react. The primary goal of the Silent Treatment is to provoke a reaction from you. Maintain your calm and control. Listening will provide you with information and necessary clues as to the triggers and underlying causes for a narcissist acting out in this way.

2. Don't try to win – it's not a competition

There's no winning with a narcissist. Even when you're 100 percent right, you'll never win with a narcissist. Retaliation will only escalate the situation. Yet don't excuse their behavior. The Silent Treatment is unacceptable, and you deserve an explanation. Focus on the goal of resolving the issue. Remember, the Silent Treatment prevents any resolution. This is your opportunity to address the issue. Try to validate the narcissist's perspective and experience. This is the path to building trust.

3. Protect yourself

Be aware of your feelings and don't undermine them. You're smart and capable. You have value. Don't let a narcissist run over you. It's important to set boundaries and limitations. Surround yourself with people who love and support you. Talk about what's happening and how the narcissist treats you. Don't let a narcissist isolate you from your support network. Receiving the Silent Treatment for long periods of time can lead to depression. Keep healthy, exercise, and meditate.

4. Seek professional help

Remember, the Silent Treatment is a form of emotional abuse. Talking about it will help. Sometimes, the best person to talk to is one you don't know who has no personal bias. This will help you work through the stress and anxiety caused by the Silent Treatment. This is for you. A therapist will help you understand what you've been through and how to prepare for other challenges.

5. Leave

Yes, I mentioned it above, but it bears repeating. After exhausting all other options, if your situation hasn't changed, perhaps it's time to say goodbye. Don't let the emotional abuse affect your mental health. Whether the relationship is a professional one, romantic, with a sibling, or even a parent, address the situation. Set healthy boundaries and limits. The Silent Treatment is one of the cruelest forms of abuse. Develop a plan and set yourself free.

WHAT HAVE YOU LEARNED?

The Silent Treatment is a form of emotional abuse used by narcissists to hurt, control, and punish their victim. For the victim, there's no way to resolve their issue or argument when the narcissist cuts off all communication. They're the target of cruelty and subsequent abandonment. You could've received the Silent Treatment from your boss, your parent, your sibling, a friend, or a romantic love. It could come from anyone.

It's not your fault. You did nothing to deserve this treatment. It's time for you to be treated with care and kindness. The first few times my father gave me the Silent Treatment, I felt confusion, abandonment, and rage. I tried all the strategies discussed above. I listened to his deflections, his gaslighting, and his hollow apologies. I tried to protect myself the best I could. I exercised, ate right, even saw a professional therapist. I only wanted peace and did not attempt to retaliate. I didn't seek revenge. I just wanted him to act like a father. We were on an unstoppable, emotional rollercoaster ride from one Silent Treatment to the next Silent Treatment climbing up steep inclines, hurtling straight downward, and careening around the corners. And to be perfectly honest, I hate rollercoasters.

13

SHOCK & AWE

"Things with my dad were pretty good until I won an Academy Award. He was really loving to me until I got more attention than he did. Then he hated me."

Tatum O'Neal

This may come across as raw because it's how I feel about what happened now and how I felt when it happened. If your feelings are raw about events you've suffered at the hands of a narcissist, I hope you can relate to mine. It's not my intention to come across as bitter, I'm just sharing my truth. As is common with narcissists, issues are never resolved.

My father apologized in his non-apology way, never explaining his actions. Until this point, the worst exchanges with him were about his insensitivity and inability to communicate with me. I thought we had some awful conversations and discussions until this betrayal.

2015 – THE YEAR OF THE PERFECT STORM

We began 2015 with the emotional grenade of the Dominican Republic. This was the first lengthy period of the Silent Treatment. At the end of February, I met with him and listened to him say he wanted his family back without addressing what happened.

He said something like, *"Was I upset about the financial commitment? Yes. Did I act like I was upset? Yes."* This was as close as he came to taking responsibility. Reflecting now, I believe the trip was Strike One to his ego.

After our return, I applied for a new job. I'd been looking for a while. My position at the hospital was fine, but I was interested in something different, outside our area, where my father wasn't as "well known." The job-hunting process began while he wasn't speaking with me, and I had several interviews. After meeting with him in February, things didn't magically improve, so I didn't share my job search with him.

In April, I was offered a new position without his advice or assistance. My father feels he's very well-connected and can call anyone for assistance at any time. It's his "Godfather" complex which goes with the narcissist characteristics listed in Chapter 2. Learning about my new job was the second blow to his ego. He didn't say anything, but he definitely needs to be needed. Clearly, I didn't need him to help me find a job. He didn't stop speaking at this point, but it was Strike Two to his ego.

I completed my final days at the hospital in May and began a new job in June. When I left the hospital, they were sad to see me go. They surprised me by telling me I'd be honored at the annual Gala in September which I established. The President of the Health System asked if I'd serve on the Board of Directors. I was flattered and honored. I thought my father would be proud. But I hesitated because things were unstable. I didn't know how he'd react. So, I waited. While at a large event, things seemed okay so, I shared my honors from the hospital with him. Looking back his response was revealing. He only said something like, *"Okay, that's nice."* We didn't talk about it again.

I didn't realize this was Strike Three to his ego. He was still missing his narcissistic supply from my mother. The culmination of three big ego strikes that year was too much. I didn't see him for two weeks. Then we both attended a large outdoor party. The first person I saw was the CEO of the hospital I left. Greg and I have remained friends and I enjoy him and his wife. After greeting Joseph and me, he asked if he could speak to me alone.

He, said, *"I don't even know how to say this, but I feel like we're friends and you should know."*

I nodded my head.

Greg told me he was approached by my father at the golf course. He asked Greg, *"Why would you ask Lynn to serve on the Board of Directors when I'm available?"*

I was speechless. No one ever told me something I didn't know about my father and certainly nothing about him opposing me. I felt like someone punched me in the stomach. I told Greg, *"I don't think there's enough alcohol at this party to process that information. Ha-ha!"* I tried to diffuse a sensitive moment when the only logical reply was to dissolve into tears. But we're at a large party with lots of people. So, I made a joke and thanked Greg for sharing it with me. It's important I know the truth, even if it hurts.

My father crossed the yard and said hello.

I was cordial, trying to keep it together. At some point, I shared with my husband Joseph what Greg said. We left the party soon after.

I don't know how you process experiences, but back then I tended to think about troubling issues over and over, agonizing over every detail. I tried to act as if it didn't bother me and just get along. But all I heard in my head was that message looping over and over again. Clearly, his ego and public image were more important than our relationship.

After sleepless nights, miserable days, conversations with Joseph and my closest friends, I decided to confront him. I had to know if it was true, although Greg had no reason to lie. I couldn't make myself meet him in person, so I called.

I tell him what Greg said at the party.

Silence. He doesn't deny it. Then he says, *"That's a misinterpretation."*

I ask, *"How so?"*

Instead of answering he goes into a blame spiral angrily spitting out that he'll never help the hospital again and won't attend events or do anything for them. He says he's been trying to cut back on his involvement anyway. He deflects to divert attention away from his words and actions by bringing up irrelevant issues. So, he gets all wound up, yelling at me. Finally, I hung up. There was no reasonable conversation to be had.

A few days later I sent him an email saying I probably shouldn't have hung up, but there was no communicating with him. I was candid about my emotions. I asked him again to please explain how what Greg told me was a misinterpretation.

He replied with an email first stating he decided not to respond. Then he changed his mind. He continued saying he didn't throw me under the bus with Greg. He said he was only kidding. This is as close as he came to any admission of guilt. Then he said he wouldn't attend the Gala in September where they're honoring me. He follows a narcissist script, playing the victim and saying he just can't do anything right, and my words are hurtful.

I wait a few days, thinking of little else. This time, his rage storm, and the emotional grenades hit hard. I feel the lowest I've felt since my mother died. I write back sharing my reactions. I point out he claimed it was a misinterpretation without explanation. Then he said it was a joke.

I reached out to Greg for a clearer picture. He told me it was definitely no joke and there was nothing to misinterpret.

MY FATHER CONTINUES:

- *He backpedaled to gaslight me about what happened*
- *He tried to make it about him, reframing the situation as a victim saying my words hurt him*
- *He directed his anger at the hospital, holding them accountable*

I desperately want him to say, *"I shouldn't have said it. It bothered me they never asked me to be on the Board. It's hard for me to realize you've achieved this, and I should be proud. I should've never said that."* But that's a pipedream, not reality.

A few days later he responded with another email. He writes, *"I made a mistake saying anything to Greg about you and the Hospital. That's my problem. I should have never said anything. Believe what you want, I was kidding him."* This is the famous non-apology apology often used by narcissists. He admits his mistake in talking to Greg but not for hurting me.

My father was a narcissist. All roads seemed to lead in that direction. He's in his 80s and missing out on being part of our family. The hospital Gala came and went without him. I couldn't believe he refused to show up. I had a hard time understanding this was because I was invited to sit on a volunteer Board, not even a paid position. However, it's a visible one, which my father covets.

I finally reached a moment when I decided the conflict was detrimental to my health and I needed to move on. So, I accepted his non-apology. He was in no hurry to meet because he didn't want to discuss it.

A month later, it hit me. I realized I'd do anything for my two daughters. If we had an argument and I said something terrible, I'd do anything to repair and salvage our relationship. My father walked away instead. His ego and vanity always came first. He showed jealousy and barely apologized. Now he was traveling, posting selfies on Facebook. He was going on with his life, while I felt abandoned.

Two and a half months after he asked that question of Greg, he changed his story again. First, it was a misinterpretation, then it was a joke. Now he sent another email:

"I do not know why I responded about the appointment. I should have never talked to him about anything to do with the Hospital and you. He brought it up. He mentioned that you were considered. I should never have kidded him—what about me.

He answered send me a resume quickly. I did not respond and never even considered doing anything because I said that to him in a jovial way not serious at all—he has always kidded with me—that was my answer—not serious."

WHAT? Greg asked my father for his resume? More lies. I asked if this was a joke, why didn't he attend the hospital Gala? Why was he angry with the hospital? Greg never asked for his resume. My father was sinking into the tactic of gaslighting; changing what happened to fit his narrative. This is exactly what we explored in Chapter 9 on Gaslighting.

Historically, this behavior has played out between a father and child before. Ryan O'Neal was an established, successful actor when he suggested his nine-year-old daughter, Tatum, play the co-starring role in the movie, "Paper Moon." The movie was widely acclaimed, and Tatum was nominated for an Academy Award. In 1974, Tatum O'Neal became the youngest competitive winner in history taking home an Academy Award for the best supporting actress at the age of ten for her portrayal of Addie. At the time, Ryan O'Neal played a doting father in front of the press, but Tatum felt his resentment grow as his performance went unrecognized.

For a narcissist, going unrecognized is enough of an ego hit. However, for a young daughter to be recognized over her parent, it's abominable. At the awards ceremony itself, Tatum attended alone without either of her parents. Many years later she reflected in her memoir "*A Paper Life*," that she felt little sense of accomplishment after what should've been a huge honor. The people she believed were closest to her didn't care.

She wrote, "The feeling I most associate with winning an Oscar is an overwhelming sadness at being abandoned by my parents—both of them ... "Years later, Tatum agreed with those who said her father was jealous, adding he was also selfish.

Ryan was a narcissist suffering a narcissistic injury. So, he couldn't attend the ceremony where his daughter was honored.

I don't receive awards often. I'm not honored by organizations every month or even every year. I didn't discover a cure for a disease or save someone from a burning building. This honor was important to me. I hoped it would be important to him.

After he said he'd have nothing to do with the hospital again – he never answered my questions. I buried my hurt. It would've been great for him to swallow his feelings and show up for me. Blaming the hospital was a ruse for not being able to handle seeing his daughter honored and refusing to take responsibility for his feelings or his actions.

Again, he exhibited behaviors like Donald Trump. In her book, *Too Much and Never Enough*, niece Mary Trump writes, "Donald's talent for deflecting responsibility while projecting blame onto others came straight from his father's playbook. ... Donald knew that taking responsibility for your failures, which meant acknowledging failure, was not something his father admired ... "

This isn't new behavior for leaders. Many leaders are reluctant to apologize. Former President Bill Clinton famously denied wrongdoing throughout his years in the White House. He never admitted or apologized for anything. During the height of the #MeToo Movement in 2017, Bill Clinton was asked if he ever apologized to Monica Lewinsky in the aftermath of their Oval Office affair and national scandal. Perhaps the years resulted in Clinton seeing what happened differently.

A Time Magazine article stated, "As the poster boss for a particularly ugly abuse of power, he had a unique chance this week to become a transformative figure ... And he blew it." So, taking responsibility for his actions meant admitting failure to Clinton. My father was incapable of doing it as well.

In the book "*The Great Santini*" by Pat Conroy and the movie of the same name, the great Santini is the character, Bull Meachum. He only understands competition, whether it's in his military unit or playing basketball with his son. He must win every time, all the time. He refuses defeat. He rejects the concept of losing completely. So, when his

18-year-old son Ben finally beats him in a game of basketball at home with the family watching, Bull refuses to accept it. He's belligerent toward his wife, the mother of their children. He tries changing the rules to make Ben play more. He calls Ben names and throws a basketball at his head, over and over.

The game is a metaphor in the movie for Bull losing precious control over his family. He's ill-equipped to deal with the loss. As a typical narcissist, he has trouble regulating his emotions and demands all the admiration and recognition for himself. Ben stands up to his father's bullying and challenges him. Then he does the unthinkable, he beats Bull. Who does he think he is?

During my interviews for this book, I spoke to Phoebe, a child raised by a narcissist. She told me that growing up she felt totally unlovable and unworthy. She never felt like she belonged or that she was good enough. Phoebe revealed she lived to have someone be proud of her and what she accomplished. She understood narcissists have no capacity to be proud of anybody. Unless, they can say, *"See, I taught her everything she knows."*

Patricia grew up dreaming of having a different father. She wished she could live with another family. She'd watch other kids in the neighborhood whiz by on their bikes while she weeded the yard. She would sit on the radiator in her bedroom, below the window thinking, "Someone please come and rescue me." Rapunzel was her favorite story. She knew she was a slave growing up as she saw other kids playing. She didn't know she was emotionally abused or how it would affect her later. Patricia thought she was living in a nightmare.

She was relieved when her mother told her she was going to leave her father. She wanted so badly to go with her. But that wasn't meant to be. Much later in her life, she told me she never forgot the day her dad died. She was sad he died and never really lived but, yet she was also relieved.

To figure out a way to manage my life with less rage and more joy, I looked for outlets. I needed to strategize how to peacefully co-exist with my father. I went to a professional for therapy. I took Zumba and kick-boxing classes. I also read the book, *"The Four Agreements,"* by Don Miguel Ruiz. It's a transformational code of conduct based on the rules of ancient Toltec wisdom.

THE FOUR AGREEMENTS ARE:

1. Be impeccable with your word.
2. Don't take anything personally.
3. Don't make assumptions.
4. Always do your best.

These agreements seem basic, but they're actually an incredible expression of high emotional intelligence. This is the ability to recognize, understand and manage our own emotions. It's also recognizing, understanding, and influencing the emotions of others. These four agreements help us communicate better and learn to understand other people. When you choose to not take anything personally, rather than feel hurt or angry you become more empowered. You are being proactive rather than a victim of another person's narcissism.

The first agreement is about using your words responsibly and taking responsibility for your actions. Everything we manifest is in our word. Be precise and intentional with your words. Listen more than we speak. According to the Greek philosopher, Epictetus, "We have two ears and one mouth so that we can listen twice as much as we speak." Practicing reflective listening is another important part of emotional intelligence and helps exhibit empathy.

The second agreement is about respect, understanding you're not the only person on the planet, not everything is about you. If you make a habit to not take things personally, anger, jealousy, envy and even sadness will disappear as a result. You'll gain empathy, compassion, and respect. These are all great transformational characteristics.

The third agreement explores the notion by not assuming, you don't come to wild conclusions without evidence. This reminds me of the quote, "You probably wouldn't worry about what other people think of you if you could know how seldom they do," by Olin Miller.

Ruiz emphasizes it's myopic to assume everyone thinks and feels how we think and feel. Stop making assumptions and ask more questions to get a clearer understanding. Better communications leave no room for assumptions.

The fourth agreement is the big transformation. The first three agreements won't work unless you do your best. This is about excellence without regret, excuses, or guilt. It's not about perfection. It's about giving 100 percent at your highest level to be the best you can be. When you know you're doing your best, your confidence and courage level will naturally increase. The whole point of these agreements is finding the freedom to enjoy your life without impediments holding you back.

HOW DO I APPLY THIS CONCEPT GOING FORWARD?

I continue taking each day one at a time. I keep my word impeccable. I say what I mean, and I mean what I say. I no longer say yes to everything I'm asked to do. My boundaries have become clearer. I give time and energy to positive things in my life. I do my best not to dwell on any negatives. I now think twice if I take something personally. This is perhaps the most challenging of the agreements for me. It's easy to feel a deep and lasting hurt from someone's words or actions.

These concepts help me remember that narcissists operate from a place of deep insecurity and trauma. Hurt people hurt people. I find drawing on my inner resources helps me to not take words and circumstances so personally. You can tap into your inner resources by finding things that bring you joy and expressing gratitude. It sounds trite but being grateful for all we have is powerful. There are people who would trade your problems any day and see them as opportunities.

I've discovered the best way for me to not make assumptions is to be more inquisitive. I now ask people more questions. Remember, narcissists, don't like to be challenged or criticized. They never like to explain their actions. So, if they don't provide answers to your questions, they're more likely to be a narcissist. For all the other people I've asked questions of, they've revealed something honest and sometimes raw about themselves. This has led to deeper and more serious conversations.

Yes, uncomfortable conversations are hard to have but they always lead to better relationships. Narcissists don't like to reveal themselves as they live in a false reality. Unfortunately, they aren't concerned about their relationships or asking open-ended questions.

My father and I came to a stalemate which spiraled downward into him giving me the Silent Treatment which continued for months. Finally, in May of 2016, we met at his home. Once again, I accept him and resolve nothing other than to move on. This ended the Silent Treatment which began in 2015. However, I resolve to not take his words and actions personally. I resolve to be impeccable with my word and stop assuming the worst. Every day I make my best effort to keep these agreements. It's helped me maintain my stability and peace of mind.

WHAT HAVE YOU LEARNED?

There was always competition but never like this. In my mind, it seemed almost Shakespearean, biblical, but probably more like Ryan and Tatum O'Neal. I was angry, hurt, and shocked. I felt betrayed by someone who I thought was my champion when he was a competitor. This wasn't normal behavior. Parents are supposed to be proud of their children. Parents aren't supposed to be jealous of their children. My father did something I never dreamed possible, but I refused to let it destroy me and my peace of mind anymore.

When it came to finding my inner peace and eliminating ongoing feelings of rage, therapy and exercise helped, but they didn't change anything for me. I needed more. I needed to understand my own mindset and how to process everything. Reading and following the Four Agreements made sense and resonated. Putting it into practice every day of your life is challenging but the inner peace I've achieved since I began this journey is priceless.

My relationship with my father, however, was never the same again. Breaking trust is like crumpling a fresh piece of paper. You can smooth it out, but it'll never be the same again. I found a way to achieve a level of peaceful disinterest or indifference which has allowed me to have a relationship with my father with minimal contact. Similar to the coping mechanisms I recommend with other types of narcissists, little or no contact seems to work best.

14

MOVING ON - AVOID THE DEMOLITION PLAN

Jonathan Larson wrote the song "Seasons of Love" for his epic Broadway musical "Rent," which he wouldn't live to see on Broadway, reflecting on a life as sung at a funeral. He wrote about how we measure a year of our life, how we quantify our joy or our sorrow. Do we count the laughter or the tears? Larson's chorus repeated the number of minutes in a year, 525,600 to be exact. He posed the question "How do you measure a year in a life? How about love?"

How do *you* measure a year? I've often thought about this concept, especially during the toughest times. I measure a year in the time I share with my husband and daughters and friends. I measure it in laughter, in experiences, in silly times, in trying times but always together. I measure a year in love. How do narcissists measure a year?

DO THEY MEASURE:

- ◦ *How many times their name was in the media?*
- ◦ *How many awards they received?*
- ◦ *How many times they were recognized casually?*
- ◦ *In revenge?*
- ◦ *In arguments?*
- ◦ *Or in taking offense?*

Being them must be exhausting and miserable. How can they focus on the positive when they're always angry or playing one-upmanship games? They feel perpetually wronged and always seeking revenge.

If time is the most valuable currency, where will you spend it? How long will you wait for your narcissist to change? The constant emotional abuse can cause physical health problems. People get sick due to endless stress. Life's too short to waste time being unhappy.

I try not to have regrets, but I've wasted too much time wishing and hoping my father would act like a father and grandfather. Holidays, vacations, special occasions, all were ruined.

While writing this book, I wanted to hear from other victims of narcissists, and I joined many online groups. They all had their own version of a wrecking ball relationship. One of the most common themes I noted was a desire to see the narcissist face karma. The victims of narcissists, wanted them to experience the same hurt, pain, anguish, we've experienced because of their words and actions. I believe narcissists face karma every day of their life. They live their lives trapped in deep insecurity. Much of their time is spent alone and miserable. They only want to control others and when they can't, they live a tragic, pathetic existence. The narcissists' biggest fear is being alone, yet their bad behaviors ironically guarantee that's exactly what they'll get. Solitude.

Some people view the narcissist as a criminal, but not like a criminal in our justice system. More like someone who uses manipulation, exploitation, and an extreme sense of entitlement to injure others. They have an intense need to control every situation, possess an insatiable need for admiration, and cannot exhibit empathy.

An article in Psychology Today stated, "never underestimate the damage that such a person can do. A narcissist is a criminal who leaves a trail of injury behind." Their image is always more important than any other person and how their actions affect someone. I believe narcissists are criminals because they steal your precious time. They take away your hopes of ever having a normal relationship. They make every pleasant experience, holiday, special occasion, or vacation miserable simply because they can. It's turds in the punch bowl every time they show up.

Narcissists are toxic people with an exceptionally low level of emotional intelligence. They never self-reflect, don't care whom they hurt, don't listen, and don't respect anyone.

Growing up with a narcissistic father, Patricia felt being obedient was love, according to both her and her siblings, they thought it was what you must do. They didn't love their dad unconditionally because he didn't love unconditionally, they were only being obedient. One day, it reached a point where her dad met with her brothers and other people to discuss Patricia and her role in the family business. He told the brothers he didn't know if he could trust her, so he decided to take away her title of corporate secretary. He also didn't think she was doing the job well or correctly, so he was also taking away her title of vice-president administration. There was no nepotism in her family. Patricia worked extremely hard for these titles and was dedicated to her job. Her younger brother knew how everything affected her mentally and physically. He told their dad, "*This will break her.*"

Her father replied, "*Let her break.*"

When Patricia learned of this, she realized she put all her eggs in the basket of someone who could and would drop them at any time or hurl them back at her. He just didn't care. Her dad didn't speak to her for two months after firing her from her position in the family business.

When he finally spoke to her, he told her how wrong she was to leave. Patricia knew she'd be physically and mentally ill if she stayed. She also knew to maintain a relationship with her father, she needed to placate him. So, she told him he was right. It was always about him – he believed that she left him, not just the business.

"One day you will tell your story of how you overcame what you went through, and it will be someone else's survival guide."

Brené Brown

WHAT YOU CAN DO FOR YOU

Once you accept the narcissist will never change, there are things you need to do for yourself. Apply the concepts in *The Four Agreements* by Don Miguel Ruiz. Live your life knowing no matter how other people act, you're consistently impeccable with your word, and not taking things personally, not making assumptions, and always giving your best. This will help you maintain your good mental health and accept what you can change and what you cannot. Their bad behavior isn't your fault. Focus on the good moments in your life.

Find ways to practice self-care. The World Health Organization (WHO) defines self-care as "the ability of individuals, families, and communities to promote health, prevent disease, maintain health, and to cope with illness and disability with or without the support of a healthcare provider." This means paying attention to you, keeping yourself healthy to the best of your ability.

A psychcentral.com article broke down self-care into three categories: emotional, physical, and spiritual. These are critical activities to help you prevent burnout, lower your stress and inner turmoil. This is as important as taking vitamins for your overall health and well-being. Don't skip it or ignore it.

EXAMPLES OF SELF-CARE ACTIVITIES:

- *Meditation or prayer*
- *Sitting in sunlight*
- *Exercising*
- *Eating right*
- *Getting a massage*
- *Laughing with friends*
- *Reading a book*
- *Having a hobby*
- *Even just putting on clean clothes*

"When we forgive and are worthy of being forgiven, we are no longer prisoners of our past."

Rabbi Lord Jonathan Sacks

Another important activity I consider self-care, especially for the victims of narcissists, is forgiveness. Forgiveness is for you, not them. It's essential you find your peace of mind. This is true self-care for you. According to the Greater Good magazine of the University of California at Berkley, "psychologists generally define forgiveness as a conscious, deliberate decision to release feelings of resentment or vengeance toward a person or group who has harmed you, regardless of whether they actually deserve your forgiveness." Forgiveness is about bringing you a sense of peace, releasing your grudges, and letting go of bitterness. This doesn't mean reconciling or returning to your former relationship. Move on and let go.

Psychology Today stresses, "forgiveness is vitally important for the mental health of those who have been victimized. It propels people forward rather than keeping them emotionally engaged in an injustice or trauma."

Forgiveness also equals freedom. Once you allow yourself to release your anger, resentment, and rage, you're finally and happily free. I was guilty of hanging on to my upset for years. I allowed my hurt and anger to continue. I let my father's words and actions run on a continuous loop in my mind. It was that pesky wrecking ball slamming into my life, crushing my emotions again. Once I made a conscious decision to accept the fact that he's ill and would never change, I realized I was making myself sick from stress. Once I was able to forgive and let go, I finally achieved my own freedom.

On the Jewish High Holiday of Yom Kippur, the Day of Atonement, there is a part of the service when we say prayers for the departed. I was fascinated to read a special prayer in the prayer book called "In Memory of a Parent Who Hurt" by Rabbi Robert Saks. No matter what faith you may be the words have meaning for all of us. It included phrases such as: *"My emotions swirl as I say this prayer. The parent I remember was not kind to me."* My favorite phrase included the words: *"Help me, O G-d, to subdue my bitter emotions that do me no good, and to find that place in myself where happier memories may lie hidden, and where grief for all that could have been, all that should have been, may be calmed by forgiveness, or at least soothed by the passage of time."* There are more of us out there, hurt by people who were supposed to care for us.

Patricia tearfully reflected her dad said he was sorry for his actions before he died. She saw him the night before he passed away and told him she loved him. He said he loved her too and he was sorry if he ever hurt her. She told him she forgave him because forgiveness rids us of negativity.

One of the coping strategies I've mentioned on these pages is to find your beacon of light, your support network. I'm grateful for my husband, Joseph, and his countless hours of listening. He only gave me his opinion if it was requested. I'm also grateful to Tina, Julie, and Liz who listened to me, cried with me, and hugged me (lots). As my daughters grew older and became more inquisitive about their grandfather and my relationship with him, they both became part of my support network. Your friends and family will often serve as your beacon to shine a light, as this behavior isn't normal. They will become outraged along with you, which is both comforting and empowering. Narcissists like to isolate you from your people. They don't want you telling anyone about their abusive ways. They need to control the narrative, so their image remains untarnished.

DO WHAT'S RIGHT FOR YOU

To proceed with your new plan of recognition, self-care, and forgiveness, it's imperative to create space in your mind to see narcissism as a mental illness and the narcissist in your life as mentally ill. Even if they'll never be formally diagnosed and won't admit to their problem, you need to remember it has nothing to do with you.

Plato said, "The highest form of knowledge is empathy, for it requires us to suspend our egos and live in another's world." This is a journey away from bitterness, shame, guilt, anger, resentment, disappointment, and shock to be better, more accepting, and arrive at a place where there's a space for their illness.

Years ago, after listening to my troubles, the Rabbi of our congregation at the time said if my father was physically handicapped, I would have sympathy for him. Since his handicap is mental, I do not. It's more difficult to sympathize with someone who hurts you regularly and with purpose. I'm trying. Healing with long-term trauma takes time. Be patient with yourself and give yourself some grace.

IF YOU DECIDE TO STAY

Perhaps staying with the narcissist in your life is temporary. Maybe you like the company, need the benefits, or the money. Sometimes you stay if you're co-parenting, and the children are young.

ONCE YOU DECIDE IF YOU WANT TO CONTINUE THE RELATIONSHIP WITH A NARCISSIST, THERE ARE A FEW MUST-DOS TO PEACEFULLY CO-EXIST:

1. Don't challenge them. This means don't question their words or actions. This also means following their directions without objection.

2. Embrace their style of communication. You already know what makes them calm and what upsets them. If you want calm, it will be on their terms.

3. Avoid arguments. Don't let them push your buttons. They know what upsets you, too. They're looking for a reaction, don't give it to them.

OR ...

The other alternative is to choose to go no contact with your narcissist. This is a last resort choice after trying to make the relationship work. Narcissists can't change, they see nothing wrong with their actions. Stop thinking they'll change. Never let a person get comfortable disrespecting you. I had to learn my father will never become what I wanted as a father. This can be extremely difficult. Grieve the loss of the relationship and even the loss of whom you thought the person was to you. Protect yourself and take care of you. Take a deep breath. Lean on your support network. Take back your power.

By the time you reach a point where you decide to go no contact, you've probably been pushed beyond your limits, because the narcissist has crossed your boundaries. You can't take it anymore. You're finally emotionally ready to let go.

They aren't normal, nor do they have normal reactions. That's why no contact is best.

People who've never experienced this pattern of emotional abuse don't understand the toll it takes on our physical, mental, and emotional selves. We've spent years, perhaps an entire lifetime walking on eggshells afraid of upsetting the narcissist. We're finally free.

HOW HAVE YOU GROWN?

"God gave Adam a secret—and that
secret was not how to begin,
but how to begin again."

Elie Wiesel

Think back to a time when you were incredibly joyful, can you remember that? If you can, you have the ability to bring back some joy in your life and feel the freedom as a positive. If you can't remember a time when you were truly joyful, you can still get there but it might take a little longer. I hope you've gained from this journey and approach the narcissist in your life with this new knowledge. Hey, you're free, it's time to dream again. It's time to enforce your boundaries and find your joy. I want you to cleanse yourself of the toxic narcissist in your life. Perhaps you've avoided this person entirely or learned how to protect your mental health while co-existing with your narcissist.

I want you to experience the pure, wholesome, authentic feelings you felt while watching fireworks. Especially on a holiday or at the happiest place on earth, when all you're thinking about is the lights, the spectacle, the sounds, and feelings of happiness. I wish you this release, this freedom. I wish for you all the things you haven't been able to think about or consider due to the iron grip the narcissist has on your life. Learn to love yourself and become your authentic self again. Discover who you are without the narcissist. One of the best gifts you can give yourself is to learn the benchmarks of healthy relationships. Learn how to resist your attraction to toxic people. It may take time.

What you allow will continue. Learn to let it go. These are the narcissist's issues, not yours. If you remove your tendency toward ownership, you can learn and move on. Let it go. This isn't about someone who hurt you once and made a mistake. This is a pattern of repeated emotional abuse. You can forgive, as you break the cycle. Victims of narcissists are conditioned over time to accept emotional abuse and outright destructive behavior as normal. *"That's just dad. Sometimes he stops talking to me,"* they say.

It's not normal and it has a terrible impact on you. I've learned to deal with it, making my own corrections and adaptations as a result. I denied my feelings about abandonment, neglect, rejection, competition, and abuse most of my life. I always felt loved when I did what he wanted. Then I felt ignored unless he wanted something.

Throwing an emotional grenade is manipulation. Giving you the silent treatment is manipulation. Throwing a rage storm to get their way is a manipulation. Narcissists generate drama, create arguments, and cause confusion as their standard behavior. This is deliberate on their part. Why? To get their narcissistic supply (fuel) also because of the narcissist's jealousy and of course control. Stop the madness. Pay attention. It's not normal to sacrifice your mental health for what you perceive as success or a successful relationship for anyone.

To counter this emotional grenade, recognize it, don't react, or engage in their drama/argument/confusion. Do what you were planning to do. Don't let their grenade derail your plans.

After everything I went through, I needed to give myself some grace. I may have made space for his mental illness, but I didn't give much thought to the post-traumatic stress I suffered as a result. All I wanted was for him to act like my father and that was never going to happen. I needed to accept him for who he was, where he was while learning not to take things personally and set boundaries to protect myself.

Every time I meet with him, and we seem to clear the air, we experience a setback. It won't happen on the first day after we meet, but it might occur the next month or next year. When it happens, I find myself back to the same feelings of sadness, hurt, and longing for a real relationship.

My mother was and still is a massive influence on my life. At times of change, she'd reference a lesser-known poem by A.A. Milne, best known for creating the beloved literary character Winnie-the-Pooh. This was particularly fitting when I experienced anxiety about a transition – from elementary school to middle school or from high school to college. The poem is titled "Halfway Down," and focuses on a moment when a person is stuck between the top of the stairs and the bottom. The poem certainly encapsulates the feelings of anxiety which go along with success (top of the stairs) or failure (bottom of the stairs). I've felt trapped there, in the middle of the staircase, with my father, for years. Perhaps we're all halfway up or hallway down throughout our lives. However, you experience your transition in your relationship with your narcissist, make sure to take care of yourself. Follow the coping mechanisms I've suggested and know life isn't a movie with a great scripted ending. Emotions come in waves. Forgive people for yourself. Most of all, forgive yourself.

So, if you're reading this book and made it to the final chapter, you're at a point where you want change. You're ready to embrace change. So, what if you choose to look at this experience as a trauma that happened to you. But it's a beautiful trauma you've learned so much from. You now see things differently, you're more self-aware. You have the superpowers of a super empath. You feel emotions deeply and appreciate other people's emotions. You've elevated your own emotional intelligence as a result. And you won't let this happen again because you know the signs and you've been there.

Being able to recognize the signs of abuse and choose not to engage is where you will derive power. Reclaim it, right your ship, and stay on that path. Don't look back.

Appreciate this moment and how far you've come.

ACKNOWLEDGMENTS

I've always been grateful for my people but never as much as during the process of writing this book. I'm very lucky for my immediate family and the friends I consider family.

Thank you to everyone I interviewed for sharing their stories. Thank you for being open and honest about your shock in identifying the narcissist in your life and the pain they caused you. I'm so appreciative of your willingness to volunteer to speak with me. With every interview, I found myself more convinced of the epidemic of narcissism we are all facing today. I know readers will identify with you and find commonality as I did.

Perhaps these stories will serve as a catalyst for someone finding themselves in a toxic relationship to make a plan and leave.

Even as an adult, I spoke with my mother every day. Sometimes just for a minute, other times longer. She was a force. She knew everything about me. I'm so thankful for her. She gave me my inner resources and the confidence to do things like writing this book.

I met Julie during my first week of classes at Boston University. Since that day she has been my best friend. While certain times prevent us from talking frequently, we've been there for each other through some of the hardest, most difficult periods of time. We've also been able to celebrate the good times as well. I spoke with Julia Weissman Dobbelaar throughout my toughest times with my father. She always gave me good advice, listened while I cried, and made me laugh. We've always had lots in common including a very dark sense of humor and developed similar coping skills. Thank you, Jul.

When I asked Tina Barber to leave one department and come work with me, I didn't know we would develop a great, long-lasting friendship. Tina was with me after my mother's sudden death. She witnessed the day-to-day challenges with my father and was shocked and awed along the way. Tina has always been an incredible friend, providing support and confirmation things weren't right. This wasn't normal. After all these years, we are still friends. I'm so appreciative to Tina for proofreading this manuscript and for her unrelenting encouragement.

I always thought of Aunt Liz as the "fun Aunt." She was the one to take me for my first manicure and my first Broadway show. As my mother's sister, she's also the closest thing to my mother for me for the last eleven years. In my lowest points, I would talk to her for hours, crying and asking questions. She's become my historian when I recall the past. After the loss of my mother, there was space for our relationship to grow.

As a result, Elizabeth Winter Cohen became my supporter, my critique, and my proponent. Thank you, Liz, for being there for me, love you.

I've been writing as a catharsis since my mother passed away. It's helped me express myself and my emotions immensely. I've always wanted to put my thoughts together into a book. After eleven years, Denise M. Michaels came into my life and asked if I wanted to become an author. Denise became my book coach and has kept me accountable and on track ever since. Denise helped guide me in becoming an author. As an added bonus, she's become an incredible friend as well.

When I hired her company as our marketing firm at a professional position, I didn't have a clue she'd become one of my close friends. She is the absolute queen of marketing with an astonishing knowledge of promotion and branding. Thank you, Lisa Churakos, for believing in me and guiding me in my coaching, speaking, and training business. Lisa has met with me regularly and has given me immeasurable amounts of advice.

I believe people come into and out of your life for a reason. At the time we met, many of my friends were suggesting I meet her. Hope Jay recognized we had many commonalities including relationships with narcissists. I've learned even more from Hope. I'm so appreciative she asked me to be on the Board of Directors of the Center for Hope. The Center is dedicated to helping victims of narcissistic abuse and I'm proud of the work they are doing. Thank you Hope for the use of the glossary in this book as well.

My daughter, Madeline, has been an amazing listener since she was small. An avid reader, she was always interested in what I was doing. She's been in college during the writing of this book. An accomplished writer in her own respect, I trust her completely. She's been an incredible sounding board and many great discussions came out of this. She always makes time to read my work and I value her opinion. I'm so grateful for Madeline's input. Thank you, Madeline. I love you.

My daughter, Allison, has marvelous vision and creativity. She has taught me so much about technology, social media, and design. She listens to all my stories and gives practical advice. The only time I didn't listen to her was when she told me not to sing in my speeches. She's mortified but it always grabs the audience! Plus, she taught me how to make TikToks, Reels and more. Thank you, Allison, for all of your patience and time. I love you.

I know I'm lucky. My husband has always believed in me. So much so, he's been purchasing writing software and creating spaces for me to write for years. He has always been my best supporter, second only to my mother. He is a risk-taker and has taught me so much. Thank you, Joseph, for making space for me to take this risk. You are my best friend, my partner, and my true love. I love you.

My husband and my daughters have never ceased to amaze me in their unyielding support of this endeavor and my absolute champions. They've never doubted my abilities and propped me up when I did. Thank you. I love you. We are there for each other unconditionally.

GLOSSARY OF TERMS

This glossary is provided by The Center for Hope for Narcissistic Abuse of Western New York. Recently, I've had the honor of becoming part of the Board of Directors and the Vice-Chairman of the Board. I'm very proud of my association with this organization and all the good they do for people suffering from this type of abuse. While not every word defined in this glossary is used in the book, I know you'll find it helpful and informative. If you are looking for help for narcissistic abuse, please contact The Center for Hope at CENTERFORHOPEWNY.ORG for more information.

Narcissistic Personality Disorder (NPD)

The hallmarks of narcissistic personality disorder (NPD) are grandiosity, a lack of empathy for other people, and a need for admiration. People with this condition are frequently described as arrogant, charming, self-centered, manipulative, and demanding. They may also have grandiose fantasies and may be convinced that they deserve special treatment. These characteristics typically begin in early adulthood and must be consistently evident in multiple contexts, such as at work and in relationships.

Individuals with NPD will be easily offended by criticism or defeat and may react with disdain or anger but social withdrawal or the false appearance of humility may also follow according to the DSM-5. A sense of entitlement, disregard for other people, and other aspects of NPD will damage relationships. While a person with NPD may be a high-achiever, the personality disorder can also have a negative impact on performance (due to, for instance, one's sensitivity to criticism).

Researchers have reported associations between NPD and high rates of substance abuse, mood, and anxiety disorders. These may be attributable to characteristics such as impulsivity and the increased experience of shame in people with NPD. There are different types of NPD, such as Covert and Overt, and many overlapping traits with other Cluster B personality disorders such as Borderline Personality Disorder and Anti-Social Personality Disorder.

Cluster B Personality Disorders are characterized by dramatic, overly emotional, or unpredictable thinking or behavior. They include antisocial personality disorder borderline personality disorder, histrionic personality disorder, and narcissistic personality disorder. Many have similar or even overlapping traits and characteristics. People with personality disorders may act out early abuse, neglect, violence, and other forms of childhood attachment failures. Codependents with a consistent pattern of dysfunctional helping are often attracted to cluster b disordered people because they are "bottomless pits" of need, which can contribute to the development of dysfunctional helping relationships and abuse.

Narcissistic Abuse is a form of emotional abuse projected by a narcissist on to another individual. Although narcissistic abuse is primarily focused on emotional and psychological abuse, there are other types of narcissistic abuse that can include abuses such as financial, spiritual, sexual, and physical. Narcissistic abuse occurs in relationships where the narcissistic person tends to seek out an empathetic partner (co-dependent) in order to gain admiration of their own attributes and feelings of power and control. The narcissist creates a dynamic abuser and victim relationship through a cycle of abuse, resulting in traumatic bonding that makes it hard for their partner to leave the increasingly abusive relationship.

Cycle of Abuse The primary model that has been offered for how narcissists abuse their partners is the three-stage idealize-devalue-discard narcissistic abuse cycle. It begins with a honeymoon stage called "love bombing."

Love Bombing involves being showered with affection, gifts, and promises for the future with someone making you believe you may have discovered love at first sight. The relationship will then deteriorate into the devaluation stage of severe and persistent emotional abuse, including gaslighting, emotional manipulation, verbal abuse, social isolation, and silent treatments which all lead a victim to become trauma bonded to their abuser. The victim will then suffer the eventual discard when the abuser abandons the victim in a cruel and dramatic fashion. This cycle can continue over and over until the victim decides to end the abusive relationship by going no contact.

Emotional Abuse is an attempt to control, in just the same way that physical abuse is an attempt to control another person. The only difference is that the emotional abuser does not use physical hitting, kicking, pinching, grabbing, pushing, or other physical forms of harm. Rather the perpetrator of emotional abuse uses emotion as his or her weapon of choice. Some examples are constant criticism, shaming, and blaming with hostile sarcasm or outright verbal assault, the use of shaming and belittling language, and verbal abuse such as name-calling, and withholding affection as punishment.

Emotional Manipulation is an emotionally unhealthy psychological strategy used by people who are incapable of asking for what they want and need in a direct way. They undermine your faith in your grasp of reality, their actions don't match their words, they are experts at doling out guilt and they claim the role of the victim.

Power and Control Narcissism is almost entirely about gaining control over others. The narcissistic personality and its obsessive desire for control is not about control just for control's sake, but an essential defense against the risk of receiving a narcissistic injury; a blow to the ego or self-esteem. Abusers use a combination of several different tactics to maintain power and control.

- *Coercion and threats*
- *Intimidation*
- *Emotional abuse*
- *Isolation*
- *Minimizing, denying, and blaming*
- *Using children*
- *Economic abuse*
- *Male privilege*

Trauma Bonds

Trauma Bonds refer to a state of being emotionally attached not to a kind friend or family member, but to an abuser. It is a negative form of bonding as it keeps you loyal to a destructive situation. The abuser uses cycles of abuse and then some form of reward to keep you trapped psychologically and emotionally. Some signs of trauma bonding are you feel stuck and powerless in the relationship but try to make the best of it. Deep down there are moments you don't even know if you like or trust the other person, but you can't leave. You have tried to leave, but you feel physically ill if you do, or like you will die or your life will be destroyed. The other person constantly lets you down but you still believe their promises. It may also be referred to as Stockholm Syndrome which is a condition in which hostages develop a psychological alliance and positive feelings and loyalty toward their captors during captivity.

Co-Dependency is an emotional and behavioral condition that affects an individual's ability to have a healthy, mutually satisfying relationship. It is also known as "relationship addiction" because people with codependency often form or maintain relationships that are one-sided, emotionally destructive, and/or abusive. Codependents have good intentions. They try to take care of a person who is experiencing difficulty, but the caretaking becomes compulsive and defeating. Co-dependents often take on a martyr's role and become "benefactors" to an individual in need. Codependents often form or maintain relationships that are one-sided, emotionally destructive, and/or abusive.

Co-Dependent Addiction has been referred to as "relationship addiction" or "love addiction." The focus on others helps to alleviate our pain and inner emptiness, but in ignoring ourselves, it only grows. This habit becomes a circular, self-perpetuating system that takes on a life of its own. Our thinking becomes obsessive, and our behavior can be compulsive, despite adverse consequences. Examples might be calling a partner or ex we know we shouldn't, putting ourselves or values at risk to accommodate someone, or snooping out of jealousy or fear.

Boundaries are an imaginary line that separates me from you. They separate your physical space, your feelings, needs, and responsibilities from others. Your boundaries also tell other people how they can treat you – what's acceptable and what isn't. Without boundaries, people may take advantage of you because you haven't set limits about how you expect to be treated. Healthy emotional boundaries mean you value your own feelings and needs and you're not responsible for how others feel or behave. Boundaries allow you to let go of worrying about how others feel and places accountability squarely with the individual.

Narcissistic Projection

is a defense mechanism commonly used by abusers, including people with narcissistic or borderline personality disorder and addicts. Basically, they say, "It's not me, it's you!" When we project, we are defending ourselves against unconscious impulses or traits, either positive or negative, that we've denied in ourselves. Instead, we attribute them to others. Our thoughts or feelings about someone or something are too uncomfortable to acknowledge. In our mind, we believe that the thought or emotion originates from that other person.

Blame shifting

is an emotionally abusive behavior or tactic. Abusers have difficulty taking responsibility for problems. They go as far as necessary to attribute blame for their circumstances to anyone else, even if it may sound somewhat conspiratorial. Similarly, they don't accept ownership of their emotions. They typically express both negative and positive feelings with language like, "You make me so mad." Blame may be attributed more subtly by saying "I wouldn't have to do this if you didn't do that" They also take the focus away from themselves by shifting the focus to a past perceived slight or time that you did something to hurt them, instead of taking responsibility for their behavior.

Denial usually refers to someone who fails to recognize the significance or consequences of certain behaviors. It also implies that something believed is untrue. When someone is in denial that a relationship is bad for them, what they are denying is not so much the nature of their relationship (e.g., that person is bad for me) as the feelings that are triggered in the course of the relationship. Denial is a cognitive process that is an attempt to alter our experience of unwanted or unacceptable emotions.

Gaslighting is a form of psychological manipulation in which a person covertly sows seeds of doubt in a targeted individual, making them question their own memory, perception, or judgment, often evoking in them cognitive dissonance and other changes such as low self-esteem. Using denial, misdirection, contradiction, and misinformation, gaslighting involves attempts to destabilize the victim and delegitimize the victim's beliefs. Instances can range from the denial by an abuser that previous abusive incidents occurred to the staging of bizarre events by the abuser with the intention of disorienting the victim.

Cognitive Dissonance occurs when a person holds two or more contradictory beliefs, ideas, or values, or participates in an action that goes against one of these three, and experiences psychological stress because of that. According to this theory, when two actions or ideas are not psychologically consistent with each other, people do all in their power to change them until they become consistent. The discomfort is triggered by the person's belief clashing with new information perceived, wherein they try to find a way to resolve the contradiction to reduce their discomfort.

Triangulation is when a toxic or manipulative person, often a person with strong narcissistic traits, brings a third person into their relationship in order to remain in control. There will be limited or no communication between the two triangulated individuals except through the manipulator. It may appear in different forms, but all are about divide and conquer, or playing people against each other. It is a highly effective strategy to gain an advantage over perceived rivals by manipulating them into conflicts with one another. Triangulation is the method used by narcissistic individuals to soothe and protect their ego.

Hoovering is the term used to describe a narcissist trying to re-connect with you after a time of separation. Often, this separation occurs after a time of silence between you and the narcissist. They need narcissistic supply to emotionally exist. They need to know that they are affecting someone, or someone hasn't got over them. They tend to keep multiple sources of supply as backup. The "hoover maneuver" usually begins after the narcissist has left you and after a period of silence. They send you messages pretending nothing hap-pened or use the pretext of a special occasion to make contact. It is very important not to respond to a hoover because it will reignite the cycle of abuse.

Intermittent Reinforcement is when a narcissist creates fear

in the victim of losing the relationship during the devaluation phase, but then relieves it periodically with episodes of love and attention. Intermittent reinforcement is a pattern of cruel, callous treatment mixed in with random bursts of affection. The abuser hands out "rewards" such as affection, a compli-ment, or gifts sporadically and unpredictably throughout the abuse cycle. Intermittent reinforcement causes the victim to perpetually seek the abuser's approval while settling for the crumbs of their occasional positive behavior, in the hopes that the abuser will return to the idealization phase of the relationship. Like a gambler at a slot machine, victims are unwittingly "hooked" to play the game for a potential win, despite the massive losses.

Silent Treatment The silent treatment is a form of emotional

abuse typically employed by people with narcissistic ten-dencies. It is designed to (1) place the abuser in a position of control; (2) silence the target's attempts at assertion; (3) avoid conflict resolution/personal responsibility/compromise; or (4) punish the target for a perceived ego slight. The result of the silent treatment is exactly what the person with narcissism wishes to create: a reaction from the target and a sense of control.

The target will work diligently to respond to the deafening silence. He or she may frequently reach out to the narcissistic person via email, phone, or text and is ignored. The narcissist communicates extreme disapproval to the degree that the silence renders the target so insignificant that he or she becomes nonexistent in the eyes of the narcissistic person. It is a particularly cruel form of emotional abuse. Research has shown that the act of ignoring or excluding a person activates the same area of the brain that is activated by physical pain. The silent treatment, even if it's brief, activates the anterior cingulate cortex, the part of the brain that detects physical pain.

Social Isolation

is often used to facilitate power and control over someone for an abusive purpose. Isolation reduces the opportunity of the victim to be rescued or escape from the abuse. It also helps disorientate the victim and makes her more dependent on the abuser. The degree of power and control over the victim is contingent upon the degree of their physical or emotional isolation. Social isolation usually begins with wanting the victim to spend time with only the abuser and not his or her family, friends, or co-workers. The abuser will then slowly isolate the victim from any person who is a support to her. He dictates who she can talk to and is often jealous and unreasonable. Any attempt to seek outside support will be met by anger and punishment.

Pathological Lying

Narcissists view other people as objects and feel completely justified in exploiting them. Lying is integral to impression management and mirroring. Lies enable narcissists to present false images of themselves to potential targets. A pathologically lying narcissist knows what is 'right' and 'wrong' yet doesn't care and will use whatever methods necessary to secure narcissistic supply. It is of no consequence to the narcissist that their lies would hurt you if you knew about them. They lie through evasion and by withholding information. They lie as a form of gaslighting, in order to increase their control over their targets by making them constantly question themselves. They often repeatedly tell the ultimate lie, that they "love" their targets. And they lie just for the fun of it.

Narcissistic Injury occurs when narcissists react negatively to perceived or real criticism or judgment, boundaries placed on them, and/or attempts to hold them accountable for harmful behavior. The bubbling up, or surfacing, of injury to the narcissist's ego manifests itself as feelings of rage and vindictive hatred for the instigator of the narcissistic injury. Narcissistic injuries are disassociated feelings of self-hatred and self-loathing that are projected onto the offending person, by either an angry tirade, cruel and vindictive verbal abuse, physical violence, or the silent treatment.

Narcissistic Supply refers to those people who provide a constant source of attention, approval, adoration, admiration, etc., for the narcissist. The attention they receive from the supply is vital for the survival of the narcissist, without it they would die (either physically or metaphorically), because their

weak ego depends on it in order to regulate their unstable self-worth and self-esteem. The narcissist is engaged in constant *self-avoidance, and narcissistic supply is their drug.*

The narcissist's inner being (the True Self) is damaged. When the cracks appear and the abuse begins, this is the real person you meet. The inner self has been trapped within accumulated childhood wounds that the narcissist has tried to divorce him or herself from. Narcissistic supply is the distraction. *Never learning in childhood* to be resilient or self-soothe, narcissists develop no conscience or empathy. They do not love themselves, others, or life itself. This is the basis of all addictive behavior. A separation from self-worth, self-love, and the ability to inwardly, emotionally navigate life healthily.

Narcissistic Mirroring

because early childhood circumstances prevent narcissists from establishing a stable sense of identity and self-worth, narcissists look to external sources for definition and esteem. When they find a prospective or new partner, they study that person and attempt to reflect their personality, style, interests, and values. People with NPD engage in narcissistic mirroring for three primary reasons:

1. They lack a stable identity and are trying on yours.

2. They are working to win you over, reflecting what they think you want to see.

3. They are faking intimacy because they lack the skills and desire for genuine connection.

Narcissistic FOG is an acronym that stands for Fear, Obligation, and Guilt. Narcissists use FOG to keep their targets in a haze so they can't see how the narcissist is using their emotions against them in order to make them doubt their own judgment and perceptions, thereby gaining complete control over them.

Narcissistic Word Salad the first most overt sign of 'narc speak' in action, is the nonsense that comes out of their mouth. It is the very epitome of verbal chaos. You will find a bunch of unrelated words and concepts all smooshed together, including contradictions and disjointed phrases, or random irrelevant and impromptu comments thrown at you. The effect and very deliberate purpose of this is to leave you entirely unable to follow the narcissist, to stop trusting your own logic, and become unable to hold them accountable for their behavior.

No Contact means that you know there is no point going around in a three-ring circus of arguments with the narcissist anymore. It means that you know you have no choice other than to end the relationship because it is not getting better, resolution isn't ever going to be reached, and that there is simply no point in trying – because nothing works. You need to block them from all social media, email and phone and make a commitment to yourself that you won't respond to a hoover. No contact is the only way to break the codependent addiction and stop the cycle of abuse.

Modified No Contact (Grey Rock) The grey rock method is

a practice where an individual becomes emotionally non-responsive, boring, and virtually acts like a rock. Emotional detachment serves to undermine a narcissist's attempts to lure and manipulate, causing them to grow uninterested and bored It is generally recommended for people who have children with a narcissist and can't go full no contact because of an ongoing need to communicate.

Flying Monkeys are the individuals that a narcissist will

recruit and then use to do their bidding, typically to isolate, alienate, and harass another person. This happens when a relationship with a narcissist comes to an end. The narcissist will tell anyone close to the couple – friends, family members, sometimes even the family members of the ex – typically false information that will turn them against the narcissist's ex-partner or even result in the flying monkeys harassing the ex-partner, alienating, or isolating the ex-partner, and leaving the ex-partner feeling lost, hurt, and in some cases, traumatized.

Smear Campaign is the narcissist's scorched-earth policy,

leaving nothing but the burned wreckage of relationships and, sometimes, reputations. The smear campaign is born out of a combination of factors, including the need to be right and have his or her "truth" become the prevailing script, retaining status and standing making sure that his or her inner hidden shame doesn't become public, and maintaining control of his or her image.

Narcissistic Entitlement refers to a belief that one's importance, superiority, or uniqueness should result in getting special treatment and receiving more resources than others. It also includes a willingness to demand this special treatment or extra resources.

Trickle Truths means that the narcissist is continuing to lie and continuing to behave in damaging, disrespectful, and self-serving ways all while claiming they are being honest with you. The narcissist withholds damaging information and presents a façade of truth while the victim continues to feel unbalanced. The victim begins to find that the details do not corroborate, or their recollection is different to the new truth being presented to them, or they discover some tangible piece of evidence that clearly unearths another lie.

We offer legal advocacy, mental health counseling, financial advisement, and holistic healing services because we want to help you build your strength in every area of your life.

Hope, Help & Healing from Narcissistic Abuse
(716) 955.9658 info@centerforhopewny.org

RESOURCE GUIDE

CHAPTER 1

- "Split in Sheehan Ranks." *The Evening Post* [NY, NY], 3 Oct. 1903, Column 1 sec., p. 3. "You can't hand us over to Tammany," said one of the bolting members. "I want to tell Sheehan and the rest of his friends that you can't spit in our faces and then tell us it's raining. We are on to your game." Published on Old Fulton NY Post Cards https://www.fulton-history.com/fulton.html

- Lowrey, Sassafras. "Putting the Self in Self-Publishing." *Publishers Weekly*, 9 July 2021. https://www.publishersweekly.com/pw/by-topic/authors/pw-select/article/86851-putting-the-self-in-self-publishing.html

- *Beaches*. Directed by Garry Marshall, Touchstone Pictures, 1988.

- *Punk'd*. MTV, 2003.

- Hoffman, Jan. "Here's Looking at Me, Kid." *New York Times* [NY, NY], 20 July 2008. https://www.nytimes.com/2008/07/20/fashion/20narcissist.html

- Achenbach, Joel. "How would Trump do on the Narcissistic Personality Quiz?" *The Washington Post* [Washington, D.C.], 3 Aug. 2015. https://www.washingtonpost.com/news/achenblog/wp/2015/08/03/how-would-trump-do-on-the-narcissistic-personality-quiz/

- *Chicago*. Directed by Rob Marshall, Miramax, 2002.

- Trainor, Ken. "Theme Song for the Trump Reality Show." *Wednesday Journal of Oak Park and River Forest*, 3 Dec. 2019. https://www.oakpark.com/2019/12/03/theme-song-for-the-trump-reality-show/

CHAPTER 2

- Eliot, T. S. *The Cocktail Party*. New York City, Harcourt, Brace and World, 1950.

- "Narcissus- Narcissus: The Self Lover." *www.greekmythology. com*, www.greekmythology.com. https://www.greekmythology.com/Myths/Mortals/Narcissus/narcissus.html

- American Psychiatric Association, (1980) Diagnostic and statistical manual of mental disorders, 3rd edition Washington DC, author.

- Freud, Sigmund. *On Narcissism*. 1914. Vol. 14, London, Hogarth Press, 1957.

- Rank, Otto. "A Contribution to Narcissism." *Jahrbush fur Psychoanalytische un Psychopathologische Forschungen*, vol. 3, 1911, pp. 401-26.

- Kohut, H. "Forms and transformations of narcissism." *Journal of the American Psychoanalytic Association*, vol. 14, 1966, pp. 243-72.

- Ronningstam, Elsa. "Narcissistic Personality Disorder." *Oxford Textbook of Psychopathology*, 2nd ed., New York City, Oxford University Press, 2009, pp. 752-70.

- Kernberg, O.F. "Factors in the Psychoanalytic Treatment of Narcissistic Personalities." *Journal of the American Psychoanalytic Association*, vol. 18, 1970, pp. 51-85.

- Lyon, Lindsay. "Narcissism Epidemic: Why There Are So Many Narcissists Now." *U.S. News & World Report*, 21 Apr. 2009. https://health.usnews.com/health-news/family-health/brain-and-behavior/articles/2009/04/21/narcissism-epidemic-why-there-are-so-many-narcissists-now

- American Psychiatric Association, (2000) Diagnostic and statistical manual of mental disorders, 4th edition Washington DC, author.

- Ronningstam, Elsa, and Igor Weinberg. "Narcissistic Personality Disorder: Progress in Recognition and Treatment." *FOCUS The Journal of Lifelong Learning in Psychiatry*, vol. 11, no. 2, Mar. 2013, pp. 167-77. DOI:10.1176/appi.focus.11.2.167

- "Narcissistic personality disorder - Symptoms and causes." *www.mayoclinic.org*, The Mayo Clinic, www.mayoclinic.org. Accessed 11 Dec. 2021. https://www.mayoclinic.org/diseases-conditions/narcissistic-personality-disorder/symptoms-causes/syc-20366662

- American Psychiatric Association, (2013) Diagnostic and statistical manual of mental disorders, 5th edition Washington DC, author.

- Salovey, Peter, and John D. Mayer. "Emotional Intelligence." *Imagination, Cognition, and Personality*, vol. 9, no. 3, 1989, pp. 185-211. https://doi.org/10.2190/DUGG-P24E-52WK-6CDG

- Goleman, Daniel. *Emotional Intelligence: Why It Can Matter More than IQ*. New York City, Bantam Books, 1996

- "The Meaning of Emotional Intelligence." *The Meaning of Emotional Intelligence*, www.ihhp.com. Accessed 10 Dec. 2021. https://www.ihhp.com/meaning-of-emotional-intelligence/

- Crump, James. "Melania Reportedly Called Donald Trump After Every Rally to Tell Him How 'wonderful and great' he is." *The Independent* [London], 1 Feb. 2021. https://www.independent.co.uk/news/world/americas/us-politics/melania-trump-donald-trump-call-rally-b1795869.html

- Ansell, Mark. "The Importance of Emotional Intelligence in Effective Leadership." *www.linkedin.com*, 3 Oct. 2016, www.linkedin.com/pulse/importance-emotional-intelligence-effective-mark-ansell/.

- Wu, Dan. "The Secret Behind Richard Branson's Emotional Intelligence." *www.gorocktheboat.com*, 13 Mar. 2020, www.gorocktheboat.com/post/the-secret-behind-richard-branson-s-emotional-intelligence.

- Alford, Henry. "Is Donald Trump Actually a Narcissist? Therapists Weigh In!" *Vanity Fair*, 11 Nov. 2015. https://www.vanityfair.com/news/2015/11/donald-trump-narcissism-therapists

CHAPTER 3

- "It is not attention that the child is seeking, but love. - Sigmund Freud." *www.quotemaster.org*, www.quotemaster.org/qa39e3188917c1707bdee8800069bf476. Accessed 18 Dec. 2021.

- Ward, Marguerite, and Rachel Gillet. "Science Says Parents of Successful Kids Have These 24 Behavioral Things in Common." *Business Insider*, 2 Sept. 2020. https://www.businessinsider.com/how-parents-set-their-kids-up-for-success-2016-4

- Glosson, Megan. "How to Know if You're an Emotionally Available Mother." *www.moms.com*, 19 July 2020, www.moms.com. Accessed 11 Dec. 2021. https://www.moms.com/signs-emotionally-available-mother/

- Hill, Tamara. "10 Signs of Having an Emotionally Unstable/Unavailable Parent." *www.psychcentral.com*, 24 Jan. 2018, www.psychcentral.com. Accessed 11 Dec. 2021. https://psychcentral.com/blog/caregivers/2018/01/10-signs-of-having-an-emotionally-unstable-unavailable-parent#1

- Trump, Mary L. *Too Much and Never Enough How My Family Created the World's Most Dangerous Man*. Simon & Schuster, 2020.

- Derhally, Lena Aburdene. "How (and why) to Create Emotional Safety for Our Kids." *The Washington Post* [Washington, DC], 23 Mar. 2016. https://www.washingtonpost.com/news/parenting/wp/2016/03/23/how-and-why-to-create-emotional-safety-for-our-kids/

- Walansky, Aly. "Narcissistic Children Have Parents Who Do These Things–How Not to Raise a Narcissist." *www.goalcast.com*, 27 Aug. 2020, www.goalcast.com. Accessed 11 Dec. 2021. *https://www.goalcast.com/2020/08/27/narcissistic-children-parenting-style-mistakes/*

- Hamaker, Sarah. "How to Nip Narcissism in the Bud." *The Washington Post* [Washington, DC], 11 Mar. 2015. https://www.washingtonpost.com/news/parenting/wp/2015/03/11/7-ways-to-nip-narcissism-in-the-bud/

- Salinger, J.D. *The Catcher in the Rye*. Little, Brown, 1951.

- Shaw, Daniel. *Traumatic Narcissism: Relational Systems of Subjugation*. New York City, Routledge, Taylor & Francis Group, 2014.

CHAPTER 4

- Lee, Harper. *To Kill a Mockingbird*. 1960.

- "Definition of Inner Resources." *Cambridge Dictionary*. *Cambridge Dictionary*, dictionary.cambridge.org. Accessed 18 Dec. 2021. https://dictionary.cambridge.org/us/dictionary/english/have-inner-resources?q=inner+resources

- *Veep*. Directed by Armando Iannucci, HBO, 2021.

- *Mean Girls*. Directed by Mark Waters, Paramount Pictures, 2004.

CHAPTER 5

- Shakespeare, William. *King Lear*. 1564-1616. Dramatic Play.

   "But yet thou art my flesh, my blood, my daughter –
   Or rather a disease that's in my flesh,
   Which I must needs call mine. Thou art a bile,
   A plague-sore or embossed carbuncle,

In my corrupted blood. (Act 2, Scene 4,.218-25)

⊚   Lemire, Jonathan. "Analysis: Trump's Rage Ignites Mob Assault on Democracy." *APNEWS.COM*, 7 Jan. 2021 Accessed 7 Jan. 2021. https://apnews.com/article/us-capi-tol-stormed-287c0c48135eebf189e02c4df4286863

⊚   Dickinson, Tim. "I Stayed Up Past Midnight to Watch Mike Pence Eat Shit, and It Was Beautiful." *Rolling Stone*, 7 Jan. 2021. https://www.rollingstone.com/politics/politics-news/pence-loss-certification-trump-rage-1111051/

⊚   Peters, Gerhard, and John. T. Woolley. "Donald J. Trump, Tweets of January 6, 2021." *The American Presidency Project*, UCSB, 6 Jan. 2021, www.presidency.ucsb.edu. https://www.presidency.ucsb.edu/documents/tweets-january-6-2021

⊚   Parker, Ashley, et al. "Six Hours of Paralysis: Inside Trump's Failure to Act After a Mob Stormed the Capitol." *The Washington Post* [Washington, DC], 11 Jan. 2021. https://www.washingtonpost.com/politics/trump-mob-fail-ure/2021/01/11/36a46e2e-542e-11eb-a817-e5e7f8a406d6_story.html

⊚   Burton, Neel. "Beyond Good and Evil Painting the World in Black and White is to Lose its Color. So why do we do it?" *Psychology Today*, 22 Apr. 2013. https://www.psychologyto-day.com/us/blog/hide-and-seek/201304/beyond-good-and-evil

CHAPTER 6

⊚   Schwartz, Daniel Mark. "Best Quotes About Narcissistic Bosses." *Overcoming Toxic People*, overcomingtoxicpeople.com/. Accessed 2020. https://overcomingtoxicpeople.com/Narcissists/Best_Quotes_About_Narcissistic_Bosses.html

⊚   *The Devil Wears Prada*. Directed by David Frankel, Fox 2000 Pictures, 2006.

- Grijalva, Emily, et al. "Examining the 'I' in Team: A Longitudinal Investigation of the Influence of Team Narcissism Composition on Team Outcomes in the NBA." *Academy of Management Journal*, vol. 63, no. 1, 13 Feb. 2020. https://doi.org/10.5465/amj.2017.0218

- O'Connell, Brian. "The Damage Done: Dealing with Narcissists in the Workplace." *www.shrm.org (Society for Human Resource Management)*, 23 Feb. 2021, www.shrm.org. https://www.shrm.org/resourcesandtools/hr-topics/people-managers/pages/narcissism-and-managers-.aspx

- Gandhi, Mahatma. *The Collected Works of Mahatma Gandhi*. Vol. XII, India, Government of India, 1964.

- Daskal, Lolly. "10 Powerful Ways to Deal With Your Narcissistic Boss." *Inc.*, 2 Aug. 2017. https://www.inc.com/lolly-daskal/10-powerful-ways-to-deal-with-your-narcissistics-bo-.html

CHAPTER 7

- *Monster-In-Law*. Directed by Robert Luketic, New Line Cinema, 2005.

- Hall-Flavin, Daniel K. "What is Passive-Aggressive Behavior? What are Some of the Signs?" *www.mayoclinic.org*, 20 July 2019, www.mayoclinic.org. https://www.mayoclinic.org/healthy-lifestyle/adult-health/expert-answers/passive-aggressive-behavior/faq-20057901

- "The Narcissists Are Among You with Dr. Ramani Durvasula,"Spencer, Stephan, host. *Get Yourself Optimized*. 19 Mar. 2020. *www.YouTube.com*. https://www.getyourselfoptimized.com/the-narcissists-are-among-you-with-dr-ramani-durvasula/

- Hall, Julie L. "7 Ways Covert Narcissist Parents Groom Children for Abuse." *Psychology Today*, 23 June 2020. https://www.psychologytoday.com/us/blog/the-narcissist-in-your-life/202006/7-ways-covert-narcissist-parents-groom-children-abuse

○ Fabrizio, Katherine. "5 (Subtle) Signs Your Mother Is a Covert Narcissist." *www.psychcentral.com/blog*, www.psychcentral.com. Accessed 2016. https://psychcentral.com/blog/5-subtle-signs-your-mother-is-a-covert-narcissist#1

CHAPTER 8

○ Snicket, Lemony. *Horseradish*. New York City, HarperCollins, 2007.

○ *Genesis*. Vol. 30:25 of *Old Testament*.

○ *Genesis*. Vol. 31:41 of *Old Testament*

○ Toohey, Peter. "Sibling Rivalry: A History." *The Atlantic*, 30 Nov. 2014. https://www.theatlantic.com/health/archive/2014/11/sibling-rivalry-a-history/382964/

○ Jack, Claire. "5 Tips for Dealing With Narcissistic Siblings." *Psychology Today*, 16 Aug. 2020. https://www.psychologytoday.com/us/blog/women-autism-spectrum-disorder/202008/5-tips-dealing-narcissistic-siblings

○ "Narcissism in a Sibling [How to Spot the Signs]." *YouTube.com*, uploaded by Dr. Ramani Durvasula, MedCircle, 13 Jan. 2020, youtu.be/kHeM0jJiB3U.

○ Crosley, Hillary. "Madonna Pays Tearful Tribute to Michael Jackson at 2009 VMAs Full Text of Madonna's Tribute to MJ at the Video Music Awards." *www.mtv.com*, 13 Sept. 2009, www.mtv.com. Accessed 11 Dec. 2021. https://www.mtv.com/news/1621390/madonna-pays-tearful-tribute-to-michael-jackson-at-2009-vmas/

○ Harp, Justin. "Madonna cheekily calls out one of her famous ex-boyfriends on The Graham Norton Show." *Digital Spy Newsletter*, 14 June 2019, www.digitalspy.com. Accessed 11 Dec. 2021. https://www.digitalspy.com/tv/reality-tv/a28038135/graham-norton-show-madonna-calls-out-famous-ex-boyfriend/

- Meng, Nina, and Mia Spring. "Breaking grudges, healing hearts Mia Spring '20 strives for peace by forgiving others. 'It's better to be happy than to hold a grudge from the past.'." *Foundations of Journalism*, 27 Sept. 2017, intro.wsspaper.com. https://intro.wsspaper.com/2017/09/27/breaking-grudges-healing-hearts/

- Balogun, Oyin. "Madonna's Feud and Reconciliation with Her Brother Christopher—inside Their Rocky Sibling Relationship." *https://news.amomama.com*, 19 Mar. 2020, news.amomama.com. Accessed 11 Dec. 2021.

- Roberts, Deborah, and Imaeyen Ibanga. "Madonna's Brother on His Strained Relationship with the Star Chris Ciccone Says He Was Ambushed at his Mother's Grave with a Camera Crew." *www.abcnews.go.com*, 9 June 2009, www.abcnews.go.com. Accessed 11 Dec. 2021. https://abcnews.go.com/GMA/SummerConcert/story?id=5366168&page=1

- Wayne, George. "Oh Brother, Where Art Thou?" *Vanity Fair*, 31 July 2008. https://www.vanityfair.com/news/2008/07/wayne_ciccone200807

- Ciccone, Christopher. *Life With My Sister*. Simon Spotlight Entertainment, 2008.

- *The Godfather, Part II*. Directed by Francis Ford Coppola, Paramount Pictures, 1974.

- *America's Sweethearts*. Directed by Joe Roth, Columbia Pictures, 2001.

CHAPTER 9

- Duignan, Brian. "What Is Gaslighting?". Encyclopedia Britannica, https://www.britannica.com/story/what-is-gaslighting. Accessed 14 December 2021.

- Stern, Robin, and Naomi Wolf. *The Gaslight Effect: How to Spot and Survive the Hidden Manipulation Others Use to Control Your Life*. New York City, Harmony Books, 2018.

- *Gaslight*. Directed by George Cukor, MGM, 1944.

- Sarkis, Stephanie A. "11 Red Flags of Gaslighting in a Relationship: Gaslighting is a manipulation Tactic Used to Gain Power. And it Works Too Well." *Psychology Today*, 22 Jan. 2017. https://www.psychologytoday.com/us/blog/here-there-and-everywhere/201701/11-red-flags-gaslighting-in-relationship

- *Tangled*. Directed by Nathan Greno and Byron Howard, Walt Disney Pictures, 2010.

- Grimm, Jacob, and Wilhelm Grimm. *Kinder- und Hausmärchen (lit. Children's and Household Tales)*. Germany, 1812-1858.

- *The Girl On The Train*. Directed by Tate Taylor, DreamWorks Pictures, 2016.

- *Overboard*. Directed by Garry Marshall, MGM, 1987.

- Taylor, Goldie. "Goldie Taylor—Donald Trump Defends Corey Lewandowski With Abuser's Handbook." *The Daily Beast*, 13 Apr. 2017, www.thedailybeast.com. https://www.thedailybeast.com/goldie-taylordonald-trump-defends-corey-lewandowski-with-abusers-handbook

- Trump turns blame on reporter in battery case, ELI STOKOLS, HADAS GOLD and NICK GASS 03/29/2016 politico.com https://www.politico.com/story/2016/03/trump-campaign-manager-charged-with-misdemeanor-battery-221336

CHAPTER 10

- *The Sopranos*. HBO, 1999.

- Degges-White, Suzanne. "Love Bombing: A Narcissist's Secret Weapon." *Psychology Today*, 13 Apr. 2018. https://www.psychologytoday.com/us/blog/lifetime-connections/201804/love-bombing-narcissists-secret-weapon

- "Dreams." Lyrics by Stevie Nicks. Recorded 1976. *Rumors*, performance by Fleetwood Mac. *www, pandora.com.*

- Schulz, Charles M. "Peanuts." *Minneapolis Tribune*, 1950. Cartoon.

- Stevenson, Robert Louis. *Dr. Jekyll & Mr. Hyde*. London, Longmans, Green and Co, 1886.

CHAPTER 11

- "Narcissistic Personality Disorder - Symptoms and Causes." *The Mayo Clinic*, Mayo Clinic, www.mayoclinic.org/diseases-conditions/narcissistic-personality-disorder/symptoms-causes/syc-20366662.

- Vaknin, Sam. "Dissociation and Confabulation in Narcissistic Disorders." *Journal of Addiction and Addictive Disorders*, 25 Mar. 2020.

- *Mean Girls*. Directed by Mark Waters, Paramount Pictures, 2004.

CHAPTER 12

- Schneider, Andrea. "Silent Treatment: Preferred Weapon of People with Narcissism." *GoodTherapy.org*, 2 June 2014, GoodTherapy.org. https://www.goodtherapy.org/blog/silent-treatment-a-narcissistic-persons-preferred-weapon-0602145

- Cloud, David H., et al. "Public Health and Solitary Confinement in the United States." *American Journal of Public Health*, vol. 105, no. 1, Jan. 2015, pp. 18-26. https://www.ncbi.nlm.nih.gov/pmc/articles/PMC4265928/

- *Lady Bird*. Directed by Greta Gerwig, A24, 2017.

- Austin, Daryl. "What You're Saying When You Give Someone the Silent Treatment." *The Atlantic*, 26 Mar. 2021. https://www.theatlantic.com/family/archive/2021/03/psychology-of-silent-treatment-abuse/618411/

- Eisenberger, Naomi I., et al. "Does Rejection Hurt? An FMRI Study of Social Exclusion." *Science*, vol. 302, no. 5643, 10 Oct. 2003, pp. 290-92. https://pubmed.ncbi.nlm.nih.gov/14551436/

- Hammond, Christine. "6 Ways 'The Silent Treatment' Is Abusive." *www.psychcentral.com*, 7 Mar. 2020, www.psychcentral.com. https://psychcentral.com/pro/exhausted-woman/2020/03/6-ways-a-silent-treatment-is-abusive#1

CHAPTER 13

- "Tatum O'Neal Quotes." BrainyQuote.com. BrainyMedia Inc, 2021. 14 December 2021. https://www.brainyquote.com/quotes/tatum_oneal_338461

- Fretts, Bruce. "Oscars Rewind: A Charming Win Filled With Drama and Rancor." *The New York Times* [NY, NY], 18 Jan. 2019. https://www.nytimes.com/2019/01/18/movies/tatum-oneal-oscars.html

- O'Neal, Tatum. *A Paper Life*. New York City, Harper, 2005.

- Trump, Mary L. *Too Much and Never Enough: How My Family Created the World's Most Dangerous Man*. Simon and Schuster, 2020.

- Schrobsdorff, Susanna. "Why It Matters That Bill Clinton Hasn't Really Apologized to Monica Lewinsky." *TIME Magazine*, 7 June 2018. https://time.com/5304900/bill-clinton-metoo-movement-apologize-monica-lewinsky/

- Conroy, Pat. *The Great Santini*. Random House, 1976.

- Ruiz, Don Miguel. *The Four Agreements*. Amber-Allen Publishing, 1997.

- "Epictetus Quotes." BrainyQuote.com. BrainyMedia, Inc, 2021. 18 December 2021. https://www.brainyquote.com/quotes/epictetus_106298

- "Olin Miller Quotes." BrainyQuote.com. BrainyMedia, Inc, 2021. 18 December https://www.brainyquote.com/quotes/olin_miller_389370

CHAPTER 14

- *RENT*. Directed by Chris Columbus, Columbia Pictures, 2005.

- Ashman, Leora. "Aphasia: Awareness of an Invisible Disability as a Survival Guide – Opinion." *The Jerusalem Post*[-Jerusalem], 3 Nov. 2021. https://www.jpost.com/opinion/aphasia-awareness-of-an-invisible-disability-as-a-survival-guide-opinion-683948

- Jacobs, Rabbi Margie. "Sefaria, Teshuva, Renewal, and Creativity." *www.sefaria.org*, 30 Aug. 2021, www.sefaria.org. used Elie Wiesel quote "God gave Adam a secret—and that secret was not how to begin, but how to begin again." https://www.sefaria.org/sheets/338107?lang=bi

- Barker, Eric. "· How to Deal With a Narcissist: 5 Secrets Backed by Research." *www.observer.com*, 28 Jan. 2016, www.observer.com. https://observer.com/2016/01/how-to-deal-with-a-narcissist-5-secrets-backed-by-research/

- Samenow, Stanton E. "· The Narcissist as a 'Criminal' The Narcissist is a Victimizer." *Psychology Today*, 28 Feb. 2020. https://www.psychologytoday.com/us/blog/inside-the-criminal-mind/202002/the-narcissist-criminal

- "World Health Organization definition of self-care/What do we mean by self-care?" *www.who.int*, World Health Organization, 2018, www.who.int. *who.int/news-room/feature-stories/detail/what-do-we-mean-by-self-care*

- Pratt, Elizabeth. "Self-Care Blog Article: What Self-Care Is— and What It Isn't." *www.psychcentral.com/blog*, 20 June 2021, www.psychcentral.com. https://psychcentral.com/blog/what-self-care-is-and-what-it-isnt

- Sacks, Rabbi Lord Jonathan. "The Day Forgiveness was Born." *www.chabad.org*, Chabad, 2011, www.chabad.org. https://www.chabad.org/parshah/article_cdo/aid/1726319/jewish/The-Day-Forgiveness-was-Born.htm

- Luskin, Fred. "What is Forgiveness?" *http://greatergood.berkeley.edu*, The Greater Good Science Center at the University of California, Berkeley, greatergood.berkeley.edu. Accessed 14 Dec. 2021. https://greatergood.berkeley.edu/topic/forgiveness/definition

- "Forgiveness." *Forgiveness, Apology, Blame*, Psychology Today, www.psychologytoday.com. https://www.psychologytoday.com/us/basics/forgiveness

- Saks, Rabbi Robert. "Alternative Yizkor Prayers To Say For Abusive Parents." *www.myjewishlearning.com*, www.myjewishlearning.com. Accessed 14 Dec. 2021. https://www.myjewishlearning.com/article/alternative-yizkor-prayers-to-say-for-abusive-parents/

- Coles, Jon. "Plato's Theory of Empathy." *Herald News Wales*, Apr. 2021. https://www.herald.wales/comment-news/platos-theory-of-empathy/

- Milne, A. A. *When We Were Very Young.* 1924.

HOW TO CONNECT

If toxic people have infected your workplace, bring in Lynn Catalano to help deal with the troublemakers and avoid hiring them in the first place.

Lynn's a sought-after speaker, leadership, and toxic workplace coach who motivates and inspires audiences. She's available for corporate workshops, speaking to teams, at conferences, and she coaches toxic employees. She brings in practical, easy-to-incorporate concepts utilizing emotional intelligence, reflective listening, and how to cope with toxic people. Lynn brings her message to life with a touch of humor and references to pop culture. She's an authority at identifying, navigating, and co-existing with narcissists.

"Lynn did two events for our organization, one on "reading the room" the other on identifying and managing toxic relationships. Both presentations were done so the audience was engaged, participated, and received actionable take-aways. I've received such high praise; we can't wait to bring Lynn back to speak with us again. Highly recommended!"

Andrea Ihara
Sisense
Field Enablement Manager, Senior

PLEASE LOOK FOR HER SPEAKING TOPICS AND CONNECT ON

WWW.LYNNCATALANO.COM

Instagram *@lynncatalanospeaks*

LinkedIn *Lynn Catalano*

Twitter *@LynnCatSpeaks*

Facebook *@LearntoReadtheRoom*

Printed in Great Britain
by Amazon